Boundless Trailblazers: Inspiring Stories of Real Women Throughout History

Maarja Hammerberg

Published by Maarja Hammerberg, 2023.

BOUNDLESS TRAILBLAZERS: INSPIRING STORIES OF REAL WOMEN THROUGHOUT HISTORY

First edition. November 9, 2023.

ISBN: 979-8223554622

Written by Maarja Hammerberg.

Table of Contents

Introduction: 1
Chapter 1: Ancient Pioneers 4
Chapter 2: Renaissance Shapers 13
Chapter 3: Revolutionary Icons 23
Chapter 4: Trailblazers in Science 33
Chapter 5: Women in Sports 45
Chapter 6: Icons of Literature 56
Chapter 7: Women in Leadership and Politics 88
Chapter 8: Social Reformers 91
Chapter 9: Women Entrepreneurs 102
Chapter 10: Modern Trailblazers 105
Conclusion 108
List of books to read to feel empowered 111

To my three beautiful girls,

This book is dedicated to you, Maria, Emma, and Sanna. As I share these incredible stories of women who achieved great things, I can't help but think about the amazing futures that await each of you.

Just like the women in this book, I want you to know that there's nothing you can't accomplish. Whether it's pursuing your dreams, standing up for what's right, or making your mark in the world, you have the strength, determination, and intelligence to do it all.

I hope this book inspires you to believe in yourselves, work hard, and never give up on your goals. No matter what you want to achieve in life, remember that you have the love and support of your family. We believe in you more than words can express.

With all my love,

Mommy

Introduction:

In a world that has been molded and sculpted by countless trailblazers, it's time to set the stage for a remarkable journey through the lives of incredible women who have shaped the course of history. "Boundless Trailblazers" is a celebration, a tribute, and a testament to the unyielding spirit of women who dared to dream, pushed the boundaries, and shattered the glass ceilings of their times. It's an ode to those whose tales have been obscured in the shadows, their voices silenced by the norms of the past. It's a vivid tapestry woven with the stories of the women who, across the ages, have left indelible marks on society, politics, arts, science, and beyond.

The pages that follow are a testament to the undeniable importance of highlighting these exceptional achievements and contributions. The struggle for gender equality persists, and the need for inspirational role models has never been more pronounced. "Boundless Trailblazers" offers a captivating and inspiring glimpse into the lives of women who refused to be defined by the limitations placed upon them.

From the ancient pioneers who shaped civilizations to the modern trailblazers who are changing the course of our rapidly evolving world, these women have proven that the spirit of innovation, resilience, and determination knows no bounds. Their stories remind us that throughout history, women have not just been present, but pivotal.

Chapter by chapter, we'll embark on a journey through time and across continents:

- Chapter 1: "Ancient Pioneers" will take you back to the cradles of civilization, where remarkable women from Ancient Egypt,

Mesopotamia, Greece, and China made their mark in fields such as literature, philosophy, governance, and academia. These were the women who laid the groundwork for generations to come.

- In "Renaissance Shapers" (Chapter 2), we'll delve into the lives and accomplishments of those who broke free from societal norms during the Renaissance, excelling in art, science, literature, and politics. Figures like Artemisia Gentileschi, Hildegard von Bingen, and Christine de Pizan will emerge as beacons of female resilience and creativity.

- "Revolutionary Icons" (Chapter 3) will introduce you to influential women who emerged during periods of social upheaval, including suffragettes, women in the French Revolution, and leaders of the Civil Rights Movement. These were the women who fought for the rights we hold dear today.

- In "Trailblazers in Science" (Chapter 4), we'll uncover the extraordinary contributions of women like Marie Curie, Ada Lovelace, Rosalind Franklin, and modern scientists who have pushed the boundaries in STEM fields, breaking through the gender barriers that once stood in their way.

- "Women in Sports" (Chapter 5) will celebrate the victories of female athletes who have triumphed over societal expectations and redefined the limits of physical achievement. Stories of Wilma Rudolph, Serena Williams, Billie Jean King, and Simone Biles will inspire you.

- "Icons of Literature" (Chapter 6) will introduce you to influential women writers throughout history, from Jane Austen to Virginia Woolf, Maya Angelou, and contemporary authors who continue to shape the literary world.

- "Women in Leadership and Politics" (Chapter 7) will showcase the accomplishments of women who have led nations and guided societies throughout history, from Cleopatra and Elizabeth I to modern leaders like Angela Merkel, Jacinda Ardern, and Kamala

Harris.

- "Social Reformers" (Chapter 8) will honor the dedication and achievements of women who have tirelessly worked for social reform and advocated for marginalized communities, from Mother Teresa and Harriet Tubman to modern activists like Greta Thunberg.

- "Women Entrepreneurs" (Chapter 9) will shed light on women who have excelled in entrepreneurship, founding successful businesses and challenging industry norms. Figures like Madam C.J. Walker, Oprah Winfrey, and Sheryl Sandberg will inspire you to pursue your own dreams.

- "Modern Trailblazers" (Chapter 10) will bring us into the present time, featuring a diverse range of women making significant impacts in their respective fields, be it technology, entertainment, activism, or philanthropy.

As we reach the book's conclusion, you'll be left with a profound appreciation for the strength, courage, and brilliance that women have brought to the world. "Boundless Trailblazers" is more than a collection of stories; it's a call to action, an encouragement for each reader to harness their own potential and help create a more equitable and inclusive future for all. Join us on this epic journey through history and be inspired by the stories of boundless trailblazers who defied expectations and, in doing so, changed the world.

Chapter 1: Ancient Pioneers

In the ancient world, where civilizations emerged and societies were shaped, remarkable women found their place in history despite the limitations of their time. They were the pioneers, the early trailblazers who left indelible marks on the foundations of human culture. "Ancient Pioneers" is our time machine, transporting us back to ancient Egypt, Mesopotamia, Greece, and China, where these extraordinary women made their presence felt in fields like literature, philosophy, governance, and academia.

Ancient Egypt: Where Pharaohs and Queens Ruled

IN THE HEART OF THE ancient world, the land of the Nile, women played roles of significance that defied the norms of their era. Ancient Egypt, a realm steeped in mystery, grandeur, and innovation, witnessed the rise of remarkable women who left their mark on history. Among the shimmering sands and colossal pyramids, they carved out their legacies as leaders, visionaries, and sources of inspiration.

Hatshepsut: The Pharaoh Who Defied Convention

ONE OF THE MOST REMARKABLE women of her time was Hatshepsut, who reigned as the fifth pharaoh of the Eighteenth Dynasty of Egypt. Her rise to power was revolutionary, for she not only assumed the title of pharaoh but also donned the traditional pharaonic attire, including the false beard, signifying her equal authority with male rulers.

Hatshepsut's reign brought prosperity, peace, and remarkable achievements to Egypt. Her architectural endeavors were unparalleled, as she oversaw the construction of the magnificent temple complex at Deir el-Bahri, a testament to her grand vision for Egypt. Her ambition and leadership proved that women could rule with strength and wisdom, breaking the mold of traditional gender roles in a society deeply rooted in patriarchy. She stands as an enduring symbol of female empowerment and a testament to the heights women could reach even in the most hierarchical of societies.

Nefertiti: The Radiant Queen of Beauty

NEFERTITI, THE QUEEN of Egypt during the 14th century BC, was not just a striking beauty but also an influential figure in her own right. She and her husband, Pharaoh Akhenaten, introduced a revolutionary shift in Egyptian religion by establishing the worship of the sun god Aten, pioneering a brief but significant period known as the Amarna Period.

Nefertiti's bust, discovered in 1912, is one of the most iconic representations of ancient beauty. She is often referred to as the "Great Royal Wife," and her presence in the royal court was not merely ornamental. Nefertiti wielded significant influence and was depicted in various official roles alongside her husband, breaking away from traditional portrayals of queens in the background. Her radiant image and her role in the religious transformation of Egypt continue to captivate the world, reminding us of the power and influence women could exert in ancient Egypt.

Cleopatra: The Enigmatic Queen of the Nile

NO DISCUSSION OF ANCIENT Egyptian women would be complete without mentioning Cleopatra, the last Pharaoh of Egypt. Her reign was marked by political intrigue and alliances, but her determination and intelligence shone through. Cleopatra was known for her command of languages, her diplomatic acumen, and her relationships with two of the most powerful men of her time, Julius Caesar and Mark Antony.

Cleopatra's story is a testament to her resilience in a turbulent era. Her presence on the world stage as a woman in a position of such authority and influence was groundbreaking. Her captivating allure and her strategic mind continue to inspire and mystify, leaving a lasting legacy of a woman who defied the odds and seized her place in the annals of history.

These are just a few of the inspiring women who left an indelible mark on the history of ancient Egypt. Their stories resonate through the ages as reminders of the extraordinary capabilities and accomplishments of women, even in societies deeply entrenched in tradition and patriarchy. From queen to pharaoh, these ancient pioneers blazed a trail for future generations to follow, proving that the power of women knows no boundaries and that the sands of time cannot obscure the brilliance of their achievements.

Mesopotamia: The Cradle of Civilization and Female Pioneers

IN THE HEART OF MESOPOTAMIA, between the Tigris and Euphrates rivers, a vibrant and innovative civilization thrived. Mesopotamia, often regarded as the cradle of human civilization, was home to pioneering women who defied the limitations of their era and made indelible contributions to society. These remarkable women ventured into realms traditionally dominated by men, leaving a lasting legacy of female empowerment.

Enheduanna: The World's First Known Author

AT THE CROSSROADS OF history, in the ancient city of Ur, lived a woman whose name still resonates today - Enheduanna. She was not just a priestess but also the world's first known author. Her father, Sargon of Akkad, recognized her talent and appointed her as the high priestess of the moon god Nanna at the Ur temple.

Enheduanna was a prolific writer, composing hymns and poetry that celebrated the goddess Inanna. Her works were not just devotional but also philosophical, and they contributed to the rich tapestry of Mesopotamian literature. Her compositions emphasized the interconnectedness of humanity and divinity, breaking gender boundaries in a society where women's voices were seldom heard. Enheduanna's legacy reminds us of the enduring power of female expression and intellect, transcending the sands of time.

Kubaba: The Queen of Carchemish

IN CARCHEMISH, A PROMINENT city-state in ancient Mesopotamia, a woman named Kubaba rose to prominence. She is often cited as the first known queen in history. Kubaba's reign brought stability and prosperity to her realm, and her ability to govern effectively challenged the prevailing notion that only men could rule.

Kubaba's story is a testament to her strength and leadership, breaking the mold of traditional gender roles in a society where queens were still a rarity. Her legacy underscores that women, too, could be influential rulers, paving the way for future generations of female leaders.

These inspiring women from ancient Mesopotamia were pioneers in their own right, defying societal norms and leaving a profound mark on history. Their stories, once obscured by the sands of time, are now being rediscovered, serving as a powerful reminder of the timeless strength, intelligence, and determination of women, regardless of the era or society in which they lived. Their remarkable contributions are a testament to the enduring power of women's voices, and their stories continue to inspire and resonate with people around the world.

Ancient Greece: The Cradle of Philosophy, Democracy, and Women's Empowerment

IN THE HEART OF ANCIENT Greece, a society known for its philosophical wisdom, democratic ideals, and cultural excellence, remarkable women emerged who defied the norms of their time, contributing significantly to the advancement of civilization. These ancient Greek women displayed remarkable courage, intellect, and creativity, making their mark in a society where the roles of women were often confined to the domestic sphere.

Sappho: The Poetess of Love

ONE OF THE MOST RENOWNED figures of ancient Greece was Sappho, often referred to as the "Tenth Muse." Born on the island of Lesbos, Sappho was a gifted lyric poet whose verses explored themes of love and desire. She founded a school for young women, where she encouraged the study of poetry, music, and dance.

Sappho's poetry is an enduring testament to her bold and unabashed expression of love and passion, challenging the conventional boundaries of the time. Her verses continue to inspire readers and remain a symbol of female empowerment and LGBTQ+ representation, transcending the centuries to resonate with modern audiences.

Hypatia: The Philosopher and Scholar

IN ANCIENT ALEXANDRIA, at the intersection of culture and learning, lived Hypatia, a philosopher, mathematician, and astronomer.

As the daughter of Theon, a prominent mathematician and philosopher, Hypatia was raised in an environment that fostered intellectual curiosity and rigor. She embraced her father's legacy, becoming a renowned scholar in her own right.

Hypatia was among the few women in the ancient world to teach mathematics and philosophy openly. She lectured at the Library of Alexandria, a revered center of learning, where she attracted students and scholars from across the Mediterranean. Her dedication to education and her contributions to mathematics, astronomy, and philosophy challenged gender norms and paved the way for future generations of female scholars.

Aspasia: The Influential Courtesan

IN THE VIBRANT CITY-state of Athens, Aspasia stood out as an exceptional woman whose intelligence and eloquence captivated the most influential men of her time, including Pericles, the prominent statesman and general. Although her profession was often described as that of a courtesan, Aspasia was far more than a romantic companion.

Aspasia's salon became a hub of intellectual and political discussion, and her insights and guidance had a profound influence on the political landscape of Athens. She is celebrated for her role in promoting women's education and elevating their social status. Aspasia's story reflects the transformative power of intellectual discourse and the ability of a woman to shape the course of history.

These inspirational women from ancient Greece exemplified intelligence, courage, and creativity, leaving an indelible mark on their society and inspiring future generations to challenge the limitations imposed upon them. Their contributions underscore the enduring power of women's voices and ideas, resonating through the ages as a testament to the boundless potential of women in every era.

Ancient China: The Land of Dynasties and Female Innovators

IN THE VAST AND ANCIENT land of China, the history of civilization stretches back thousands of years. Within this rich tapestry of history, remarkable women emerged as influential figures who defied the constraints of their era, contributing significantly to the cultural, political, and intellectual landscape of ancient China.

Ban Zhao: The Scholar and Historian

BAN ZHAO, ALSO KNOWN as Cao Dagu, was a prominent figure in the Eastern Han dynasty during the 1st and 2nd centuries. She was a scholar, historian, and poet, best known for her significant contributions to Chinese literature. Ban Zhao compiled the "Lesser Learning for Women" (Nüjie) a text advocating for women's education and their importance in the family and society.

In an era where women's education was often neglected, Ban Zhao's work served as an early testament to the empowerment of women through knowledge. Her scholarship and her commitment to women's rights made her a pioneering figure in Chinese history. Her influence extended beyond her time, as her works continued to inspire women in later dynasties to pursue education and intellectual development.

Fu Hao: The Military General and Priestess

FU HAO, ALSO KNOWN as Lady Hao, lived during the Shang dynasty (c. 13th century BC) and was a high-ranking military general, priestess, and oracle bone script expert. She was the consort of King Wu Ding and led armies in battle, including the conquest of the ancient state of Sanxingdui.

Fu Hao's military prowess, leadership, and religious roles were unprecedented for her time. Her tomb, discovered in 1976, contained a vast treasure trove of artifacts, illustrating her significant role in the

Shang dynasty. Her legacy highlights that women in ancient China could hold positions of great power and influence in both military and spiritual matters, challenging traditional gender norms.

Wu Zetian: The Empress Regnant

WU ZETIAN, A REMARKABLE woman who lived during the Tang dynasty, stands as one of the most influential figures in Chinese history. She was the only woman in Chinese history to assume the title of Huangdi (Emperor), ruling during a period known as the Zhou dynasty (690–705 AD).

Wu Zetian's reign marked a time of stability, economic prosperity, and cultural advancement. She instituted reforms and expanded the civil service examination system, opening up opportunities for men and women to hold government positions based on merit rather than noble birth. Her achievements in governance and her groundbreaking ascent to the throne continue to serve as an inspiration for women in leadership roles.

These inspirational women from ancient China defied societal norms and left an enduring legacy that transcends time. Their stories of intellectual and political influence, military leadership, and social reform underscore the boundless potential of women in every era. Their remarkable contributions continue to inspire and pave the way for women in contemporary society to challenge limitations and reach for greatness.

THESE ANCIENT PIONEERS were the precursors to a legacy of female empowerment that continues to this day. Their stories remind us that even in societies steeped in tradition and patriarchy, women had the strength to carve their own paths, inspiring others to follow in their footsteps. "Ancient Pioneers" is a chapter that not only brings these women's stories to life but also rekindles our appreciation for the enduring spirit of those who dared to pioneer, to break the mold, and to pave the way for future generations of trailblazers. Their stories resonate through the ages, guiding us as we embark on a journey through the annals of history, celebrating the strength and resilience of women who, in their time, were true pioneers.

Chapter 2: Renaissance Shapers

As we journey through history, our next stop takes us to the Renaissance, a period of profound transformation and creativity. This chapter immerses us in the lives and accomplishments of remarkable women who flourished during this time, transcending societal norms and breaking free from the constraints of their era. The Renaissance, which spanned the 14th to the 17th century, was marked by a rebirth of interest in art, science, literature, and humanism, and these women emerged as iconic figures who played instrumental roles in shaping the course of history.

Artemisia Gentileschi: The Baroque Painter

ARTEMISIA GENTILESCHI was a Baroque painter who defied the conventions of her time. Born in 1593, she was the daughter of the accomplished artist Orazio Gentileschi. Artemisia's talent, however, was uniquely her own. She overcame the limitations placed upon women in the arts, producing powerful and emotionally charged works that often depicted strong, heroic women.

Artemisia's most famous painting, "Judith Slaying Holofernes," reflects her skill in capturing the dramatic and the poignant. Her artistic achievements and perseverance in a male-dominated field have made her a celebrated figure in the art world and a source of inspiration for women artists throughout history.

Hildegard von Bingen: The Medieval Polymath

HILDEGARD VON BINGEN, who lived from 1098 to 1179, was a true Renaissance woman before the Renaissance. She was a polymath, excelling in various fields including theology, music, literature, and natural history. As a Benedictine abbess, Hildegard composed beautiful and ethereal music, wrote theological and medicinal texts, and created stunning illustrations.

Her "Scivias," a compendium of visions and prophecies, remains an enduring work of spiritual and intellectual significance. Hildegard's contributions were remarkable not only for her time but also for the centuries that followed, where she continued to inspire women who sought to explore the worlds of art and knowledge.

Christine de Pizan: The Pioneering Feminist Writer

CHRISTINE DE PIZAN, born in 1364, was a groundbreaking Renaissance writer and one of the first feminists in recorded history. At a time when chivalry and courtly love were the dominant literary themes, Christine dared to challenge the prevailing misogyny with her writings.

Her most renowned work, "The Book of the City of Ladies," served as a spirited defense of women, championing their virtues and achievements. Christine de Pizan's fearless advocacy for women's rights and her eloquent prose made her an iconic figure in the history of feminism and literature.

THESE RENAISSANCE SHAPERS defied societal norms, cultivated their unique talents, and left lasting legacies that continue to inspire generations of women. Their achievements in the fields of art, science, and literature are a testament to the enduring power of women's creativity, intellect, and determination. As we delve deeper into the lives of these remarkable women, we'll uncover the layers of their influence and celebrate their pivotal roles in the transformative period of the Renaissance.

38 remarkable women of the Renaissance:

1. ISABELLA D'ESTE (1474-1539):

- Isabella d'Este, the daughter of the Duke of Ferrara, was renowned for her patronage of the arts and her extensive collection of art and antiquities. Her court in Mantua attracted some of the most celebrated artists and scholars of her time, including Leonardo da Vinci, Titian, and Baldassare Castiglione.

- As a diplomat, Isabella played a crucial role in the political intrigues of Renaissance Italy. She used her diplomatic skills to secure her family's interests and maintain the stability of the region.

2. Renee of France (1510-1574):

- Renee of France, the daughter of King Louis XII, was a proponent of religious tolerance and a supporter of the Protestant Reformation. Her court in Ferrara welcomed leading figures of the Reformation, including John Calvin.

- She used her position to advocate for religious freedom and dialogue between different faiths. Her efforts to promote Protestantism in Italy left an indelible mark on the religious landscape of the time.

3. Caterina Sforza (1463-1509):

- Caterina Sforza was a formidable military and political figure during the Renaissance. She defended her family's territories, even taking up arms and leading troops to protect her interests.

- Her daring actions, including defending the fortress of Forlì while pregnant, made her a legendary figure. Her audacity and resilience in the face of adversity have inspired generations.

4. Laura Cereta (1469-1499):

- Laura Cereta was a Renaissance humanist known for her letters and essays promoting women's education and equality. Her writings reflect her deep commitment to the pursuit of knowledge and her advocacy for gender equality.

- Her work, such as the "Letter to Properzia Bardi," challenged the prevailing gender norms and established her as a prominent advocate for women's intellectual development.

5. Lucrezia Borgia (1480-1519):

- Lucrezia Borgia, the daughter of Pope Alexander VI, was a complex and controversial figure in Renaissance Italy. Her life was marked by political intrigue, marriages of convenience, and accusations of scandal.

- Her influence extended to the political realm, and she played a crucial role in the diplomatic efforts of her family. Her story has fascinated scholars and artists for centuries, serving as the basis for numerous works of historical fiction.

6. Tullia d'Aragona (1510-1556):

- Tullia d'Aragona was an Italian poet and courtesan who made a name for herself in literary circles during the Renaissance. Her salon in Rome became a gathering place for intellectuals, artists, and writers of the time.

- Tullia's poetry and her contributions to the dialogue form were notable for their wit and intelligence. She challenged the traditional roles of women, carving out a space for her voice in the male-dominated world of the Italian Renaissance.

7. Marietta Robusti (c. 1560-1590):

- Marietta Robusti, known as La Tintoretta, was the daughter of the famous Venetian painter Tintoretto. She demonstrated remarkable talent as an artist, creating vibrant and expressive portraits.

- Her works are celebrated for their vivid and engaging depictions, and she helped break the gender barrier in the art world. Her paintings showcased her unique artistic perspective and contributions to the Venetian Renaissance.

8. Lavinia Fontana (1552-1614):

- Lavinia Fontana was one of the most prominent female artists of the late Renaissance in Italy. She gained recognition for her portraits and religious paintings, working for prominent patrons.

- Fontana's successful career challenged the norms of her time. Her remarkable talent and ability to secure prestigious commissions made her a trailblazer for future generations of female artists.

9. Artemisia Lomi Gentileschi (1593-1653):

- Artemisia Gentileschi was an Italian Baroque painter known for her emotionally charged works, often depicting strong, heroic women. She overcame the constraints of her time and created powerful art that remains celebrated today.

- Her story serves as a testament to her perseverance and talent in a male-dominated art world. Her depictions of women who triumphed over adversity continue to resonate with modern audiences.

10. Madame de Rambouillet (1588-1665):

- Catherine de Vivonne, known as Madame de Rambouillet, was a prominent figure in the literary circles of 17th-century France. Her Parisian salon was a center of intellectual and cultural activity.

- Her salon attracted leading intellectuals, writers, and artists of the time, including Pierre Corneille, Racine, and La Fontaine. Madame de Rambouillet's influence on French literature and culture was substantial, and her commitment to the pursuit of knowledge made her a guiding light for intellectual women of her era.

Certainly, let's explore the lives and contributions of these remarkable women from the Renaissance period in greater detail:

11. Caterina Vigri (1413-1463):

- Caterina Vigri, also known as Saint Catherine of Bologna, was an Italian nun and artist. She became an important figure in the religious and artistic circles of her time. Caterina is celebrated for her illuminations, which were richly detailed and incorporated her deep devotion to the Catholic faith.

12. Dervorguilla of Galloway (1210-1290):

- Dervorguilla of Galloway, a Scottish noblewoman, was known for her contributions to poetry and patronage of literature. She established Sweetheart Abbey in memory of her husband, John de Balliol, and encouraged the creation of poetry during her lifetime.

13. Ginevra de' Benci (c. 1457-1521):

- Ginevra de' Benci was an Italian noblewoman and the subject of a celebrated portrait by Leonardo da Vinci. She was admired for her exceptional beauty and intellect, and her portrait is considered one of the earliest works of the great Renaissance artist.

14. Margaret More Roper (1505-1544):

- Margaret More Roper, the daughter of Sir Thomas More, was an accomplished scholar and writer. She translated and commented on the works of the Dutch humanist Erasmus, furthering the dissemination of Renaissance ideas in England.

15. Jeanne d'Albret (1528-1572):

- Jeanne d'Albret, Queen of Navarre, was a significant Huguenot leader during the French Wars of Religion. Her conversion to Calvinism and her support for Protestantism played a crucial role in shaping the religious landscape of her time.

16. Antonia Pulci (c. 1452-1501):

- Antonia Pulci was an Italian poet and writer known for her witty and satirical verses. She was a member of the literary circle of Florence and contributed to the cultural vibrancy of the city with her humorous poetry.

17. Angela Merici (1474-1540):

- Angela Merici was an Italian religious educator and the founder of the Ursuline order. She dedicated her life to the education of girls and the care of the poor, emphasizing the importance of women's education during the Renaissance.

18. Anne Boleyn (c. 1501-1536):

- Anne Boleyn was the second wife of King Henry VIII of England and the mother of Queen Elizabeth I. Her marriage to Henry VIII led to the English Reformation, which significantly altered the course of English history and the Church.

19. Isotta Nogarola (1418-1466):

- Isotta Nogarola was an Italian humanist, writer, and scholar. She corresponded with leading humanists of her time and was known for her eloquent Latin and Italian prose. Her intellect and writings challenged the prevailing norms of her era.

20. Artemisia Lomi Gentileschi (1593-1653):

- Artemisia Gentileschi, the daughter of the painter Orazio Gentileschi, was a Baroque artist celebrated for her powerful depictions of women and biblical stories. She overcame the constraints placed upon women in the arts and established herself as a prominent figure in the male-dominated art world.

21. Elisabetta Sirani (1638-1665):

- Elisabetta Sirani was a renowned Italian Baroque painter, known for her mastery of portraiture and history painting. Her talent and prolific output made her a prominent figure in the Bolognese school of painting.

22. Elena Cornaro Piscopia (1646-1684):

- Elena Cornaro Piscopia was an Italian mathematician, philosopher, and the first woman to earn a doctoral degree. Her pioneering contributions to mathematics and philosophy challenged gender norms and laid the groundwork for future scholars.

23. Ginevra Aldrovandi Hercolani (1542-1595):

- Ginevra Aldrovandi Hercolani was an Italian poet and writer, known for her sonnets and poems. Her literary works, marked by themes of love and spirituality, contributed to the cultural and intellectual tapestry of the Renaissance.

24. Lucrezia Tornabuoni (1425-1482):

- Lucrezia Tornabuoni was an Italian noblewoman known for her poetry and religious writings. She was a prominent figure in the Medici family, and her patronage of the arts helped support and enrich Renaissance Florence.

25. Isabella Andreini (1562-1604):

- Isabella Andreini was an Italian actress and playwright, celebrated for her performances in the Gelosi theater troupe. She also authored several plays and was a key figure in commedia dell'arte, a form of Italian theater that combined scripted and improvised performances.

26. Maddalena Casulana (c. 1540-1590):

- Maddalena Casulana was an Italian composer and musician, renowned for being the first woman to have her madrigals published. Her compositions during the late Renaissance were celebrated for their artistic and musical merit.

27. Vittoria Colonna (1490-1547):

- Vittoria Colonna was an Italian poet, known for her Petrarchan sonnets. Her profound influence on Renaissance literature and her close friendship with Michelangelo contributed to the cultural vitality of her time.

28. Tullia d'Aragona (1510-1556):

- Tullia d'Aragona was an Italian poet and courtesan who gained recognition in literary circles during the Renaissance. Her salon in Rome was a gathering place for intellectuals, artists, and writers, fostering intellectual exchange and artistic collaboration.

29. Mary Sidney Herbert (1561-1621):

- Mary Sidney Herbert was an English poet, translator, and patron of the arts. Her translations of the Psalms and her support of poets and playwrights in the Elizabethan era were instrumental in shaping the literature and culture of the time.

30. Gaspara Stampa (1523-1554):

- Gaspara Stampa was an Italian poet known for her passionate sonnets and madrigals. Her work explored themes of love and desire, making her a notable figure in Renaissance literature and contributing to the development of the Petrarchan tradition.

31. Veronica Franco (1546-1591):

- Veronica Franco, a Venetian courtesan, was also a celebrated poet and writer. Her poetry and letters challenged gender norms and promoted women's intellectual capabilities during the Renaissance. Her literary work explored themes of love, desire, and the position of women in society.

32. Moderata Fonte (1555-1592):

- Moderata Fonte, also known as Modesta Pozzo, was an Italian poet and writer who addressed the status of women in society and advocated for their education and equality in her works, including "The Worth of Women." Her writings challenged the prevailing gender norms of her time and contributed to the discourse on women's rights.

33. Louise Labé (1524-1566):

- Louise Labé, a French poet, was celebrated for her lyric poetry and her contributions to the Pléiade literary movement. Her sonnets challenged the gender norms of her time and conveyed themes of love, beauty, and human emotions.

34. Chiara Matraini (1515-1604):

- Chiara Matraini, an Italian poet and writer, contributed to Renaissance literature with her poetry, religious writings, and letters. She was a prominent figure in the literary scene during the Renaissance and expressed her intellectual abilities through her work.

35. Isotta Nogarola (1418-1466):

- Isotta Nogarola was an Italian humanist, writer, and scholar known for her eloquent Latin and Italian prose. She corresponded with leading humanists of her time, engaging in intellectual discourse that challenged the prevailing gender norms and contributed to the development of Renaissance humanism.

36. Laura Cereta (1469-1499):

- Laura Cereta, a Renaissance humanist, was known for her letters and essays advocating for women's education and equal rights. Her writings challenged traditional gender roles and emphasized the importance of women's intellectual development during the Renaissance.

37. Maddalena Casulana (c. 1540-1590):

- Maddalena Casulana, an Italian composer and musician, achieved recognition as the first woman to have her madrigals published. Her compositions during the late Renaissance were celebrated for their artistic and musical merit, marking a significant contribution to the music of her time.

38. Isabella Andreini (1562-1604):

- Isabella Andreini, an Italian actress and playwright, was celebrated for her performances in the Gelosi theater troupe. Her talents extended to playwriting, and she authored several plays, contributing to the lively world of commedia dell'arte.

THESE REMARKABLE WOMEN, each with their unique talents, roles, and contributions, played pivotal roles in shaping the cultural, political, and intellectual landscape of the Renaissance. Their achievements broke gender barriers and left enduring legacies that continue to inspire and empower women today.

Chapter 3: Revolutionary Icons

In this riveting chapter, we'll take a journey through history, exploring the lives of women who stood at the forefront of revolutions, social change, and the fight for women's rights. These are the fearless, determined women who defied the odds, reshaped societies, and left an indelible mark on the world.

The Suffragettes: Pioneers of Equality

THE SUFFRAGETTES, THOSE tenacious pioneers of equality, played a pivotal role in the fight for women's right to vote. Their courage and unwavering dedication to the cause set the stage for a seismic shift in gender dynamics and political representation.

The Spark that Ignited the Movement

THE SUFFRAGETTE MOVEMENT, often regarded as the first wave of feminism, had its roots in the 19th century, as women began to question their exclusion from the democratic process. Leading this charge was a formidable trio: Susan B. Anthony, Elizabeth Cady Stanton, and Lucretia Mott. These women were visionary leaders, advocating for women's rights, including the right to vote, in a society that considered such notions radical.

The Struggle Begins

IN 1848, THE SENECA Falls Convention, organized by Stanton and Mott, marked the official launch of the women's suffrage movement.

The Declaration of Sentiments, drafted at this convention, echoed the Declaration of Independence, demanding equality and political representation for women. This bold declaration catalyzed the movement and set its goals firmly in place.

The Militant Tactics of Alice Paul and the Pankhursts

AS THE SUFFRAGETTE movement evolved, new leaders emerged, introducing more radical tactics to garner attention. Alice Paul, a tireless activist, founded the National Woman's Party in the United States. She and her fellow suffragettes engaged in hunger strikes, pickets, and dramatic protests outside the White House. Similarly, in the UK, the Pankhurst family, led by Emmeline Pankhurst and her daughters Christabel and Sylvia, established the Women's Social and Political Union. They adopted militant tactics, including smashing windows and chaining themselves to railings, to demand women's right to vote. These actions, though controversial, drew immense media attention and added urgency to the cause.

The Global Impact

SUFFRAGE MOVEMENTS weren't limited to the United States and the UK. Women worldwide were inspired by the suffragettes' bravery and determination. In New Zealand, for example, Kate Sheppard led the campaign for women's suffrage, resulting in the country becoming the first self-governing nation to grant women the right to vote in 1893. Australia, Finland, and Norway soon followed suit.

Victory Achieved

DESPITE FACING FIERCE opposition and even imprisonment, the suffragettes persisted in their fight. Their tireless efforts paid off when, in 1920, the 19th Amendment was ratified in the United States, granting women the right to vote. In the UK, the Representation of the People Act 1918 granted the right to vote to women over 30 who met certain property qualifications, a significant step toward universal suffrage.

The suffragettes' legacy goes beyond the right to vote. They shattered the prevailing norms, challenging the notion that women were confined to domestic spheres. Their determination showcased women's potential as active citizens, opening doors to broader opportunities in education, employment, and public life.

The suffragettes' fight serves as a testament to the power of grassroots movements and the importance of persistence in the face of adversity. They were pioneers who left an enduring mark on history, and their stories continue to inspire generations of women to stand up for their rights and push for change, proving that progress is possible, even when the odds seem insurmountable.

Women in the French Revolution: Olympe de Gouges

AS WE DELVE INTO THE pages of history, we encounter a remarkable woman whose name still echoes through time—Olympe de Gouges. She stands as a symbol of unwavering courage and a champion for women's rights during one of the most tumultuous periods in French history, the French Revolution.

The Revolutionary Setting

THE LATE 18TH CENTURY was a time of radical change in France. The French Revolution, with its lofty ideals of liberty, equality, and fraternity, had ignited a fire of transformation throughout the country. But, as many of the revolutionary leaders focused on the rights of men, women found themselves largely excluded from the narrative.

The Proclamation of Equality

OLYMPE DE GOUGES, BORN as Marie Gouze in 1748, was a playwright, political activist, and an unapologetic advocate for women's rights. Her most famous work, "Déclaration des droits de la femme et de la citoyenne" (Declaration of the Rights of Woman and the Female Citizen), published in 1791, remains an enduring testament to her visionary spirit. In this declaration, de Gouges demanded equal rights for women, just as the male revolutionaries were clamoring for.

A Fearless Pen and an Unyielding Spirit

OLYMPE DE GOUGES WAS no stranger to controversy. Her writings, including plays and political tracts, boldly challenged societal norms. In "The Declaration," she argued that women had the right to engage in all aspects of public life, including politics. She also decried the horrors of slavery, a stance that was daring and unconventional for her time.

The Clash with Robespierre

AS DE GOUGES FEARLESSLY voiced her demands for gender equality, she found herself in direct opposition to the powerful Maximilien Robespierre, a key figure in the French Revolution. Robespierre, who had initially supported the Revolution's ideals of equality, began to view de Gouges and her ideas as a threat. In 1793, he initiated the Reign of Terror, which aimed to suppress dissent and opposition.

A Tragic End

OLYMPE DE GOUGES CONTINUED her activism despite the increasing dangers. In 1793, she wrote an open letter criticizing Robespierre's government and the Reign of Terror. Her boldness came at a high cost. She was arrested, charged with sedition, and subsequently executed by the guillotine in November 1793, a fate she shared with many revolutionaries of her time.

Legacy and Inspiration

OLYMPE DE GOUGES MAY have perished on the executioner's block, but her legacy endured. Her courageous stance for women's rights and her fight for equality earned her a place in history as a pioneer of gender equality. Her writings continue to inspire contemporary feminists and advocates for human rights. She demonstrated that even in the most tumultuous of times, a lone voice can echo through history, challenging the status quo and paving the way for future generations.

In the annals of the French Revolution, Olympe de Gouges stands as a beacon of unwavering determination. Her life and work serve as a reminder that the fight for equality is a timeless struggle, and her legacy continues to inspire individuals around the world to challenge societal norms, advocate for justice, and demand equal rights for all, regardless of gender.

Civil Rights Champions: From Rosa Parks to Coretta Scott King

THE CIVIL RIGHTS MOVEMENT in the United States was a pivotal moment in history, marked by the courage and determination of countless individuals who stood up against racial segregation and discrimination. Among these unsung heroes were remarkable women whose contributions to the movement were integral to its success. In this chapter, we explore the extraordinary stories of Rosa Parks and Coretta Scott King, two prominent Civil Rights champions whose unwavering dedication to justice reshaped the nation.

Rosa Parks: The Mother of the Civil Rights Movement

ROSA PARKS, OFTEN REFERRED to as "the Mother of the Civil Rights Movement," played a defining role in the struggle for racial equality. On December 1, 1955, in Montgomery, Alabama, Rosa Parks refused to give up her seat to a white man on a bus, an act of peaceful resistance that reverberated across the nation. Her arrest sparked the Montgomery Bus Boycott, a mass protest led by Dr. Martin Luther King Jr., which lasted for 381 days and ultimately led to the desegregation of public buses in Montgomery.

Parks' action was not a spontaneous act of defiance but the result of years of involvement in civil rights activism. She was a secretary for the Montgomery chapter of the NAACP, where she worked with other activists to challenge segregation in the Jim Crow South. Parks' courage inspired countless others and transformed her into a symbol of resistance against injustice. Her refusal to give in to discrimination marked a turning point in the Civil Rights Movement, setting the stage for subsequent struggles and victories.

Coretta Scott King: A Beacon of Strength and Leadership

WHILE HER HUSBAND, Dr. Martin Luther King Jr., was a prominent figure in the Civil Rights Movement, Coretta Scott King was an influential force in her own right. An accomplished singer, activist, and advocate for nonviolence, Coretta was an integral part of the movement's success. She not only supported her husband but also played a significant role in organizing and participating in civil rights demonstrations and protests.

After Dr. King's assassination in 1968, Coretta continued to champion the cause of civil rights and social justice. She founded the Martin Luther King Jr. Center for Nonviolent Social Change, dedicated to preserving her husband's legacy and promoting his philosophy of nonviolence. She also advocated for women's rights and

LGBT rights, recognizing that the struggle for equality extended beyond racial lines.

In 1986, Coretta King's tireless efforts bore fruit when the U.S. government officially recognized Martin Luther King Jr. Day as a federal holiday. She had tirelessly lobbied for this recognition, emphasizing the importance of her husband's work in the civil rights movement and his enduring legacy.

Legacy and Inspiration

ROSA PARKS AND CORETTA Scott King were symbols of resilience, determination, and unwavering commitment to justice and equality. Their stories remind us that the Civil Rights Movement was not solely the work of male leaders but the collective efforts of countless individuals, including women who defied societal norms to pave the way for a more equitable society.

Their contributions continue to inspire generations to stand up against oppression, promote tolerance and understanding, and work toward a world where all individuals are judged by the content of their character, not the color of their skin. Rosa Parks and Coretta Scott King's legacies remain a testament to the power of ordinary people to effect extraordinary change and the enduring struggle for justice and equality.

Sor Juana Inés de la Cruz: A Voice in Colonial Mexico

IN THE HEART OF COLONIAL Mexico, during the 17th century, a remarkable woman emerged who would challenge the constraints of her time and become a prominent figure in the realms of literature, theology, and advocacy for women's rights. Her name was Sor Juana Inés de la Cruz, and her life's story is a testament to her brilliance and unwavering commitment to breaking free from societal norms.

The Context of Colonial Mexico

SOR JUANA WAS BORN Juana Inés de Asbaje y Ramírez de Santillana in 1648 in San Miguel Nepantla, a small village near Mexico City. Colonial Mexico was a deeply patriarchal society, where women were expected to conform to traditional gender roles, mainly centered around domestic duties and piety. Education for girls was limited, and scholarly pursuits were reserved for men.

A Quest for Knowledge

FROM A YOUNG AGE, SOR Juana displayed an insatiable appetite for learning. Despite the societal limitations placed on women's education, she learned to read and write at an early age. She was known for her voracious reading and often borrowed books from her grandfather's library. Her intellectual prowess was evident, even in her teenage years.

At the age of 16, Sor Juana entered the Convent of the Discalced Carmelites in Mexico City, embracing the life of a nun and seeking refuge from the constraints of the outside world. Within the convent, she continued to cultivate her intellectual interests and wrote poetry and prose that reflected her profound knowledge of literature, philosophy, and theology.

"Respuesta a Sor Filotea de la Cruz"

ONE OF SOR JUANA'S most significant contributions was her response to a bishop's critique of a sermon she had written. In her defense, Sor Juana penned "Respuesta a Sor Filotea de la Cruz" ("Reply to Sor Filotea of the Cross"), a work of eloquence and fervor that argued for a woman's right to access education and knowledge. In this response, she asserted that women were just as capable as men of engaging in intellectual pursuits.

Sor Juana's audacious stance in defense of women's intellectual potential was nothing short of revolutionary during her time. It challenged the prevailing notions of female submissiveness and silence, confronting the deeply ingrained gender norms that relegated women to the domestic sphere.

Her Literary Legacy

SOR JUANA'S BODY OF work encompassed not only her advocacy for women's education but also her literary output, which included poetry, plays, and essays. She was celebrated for her poetic compositions, and her sonnets and love poems showcased her skill and creativity. One of her most famous works, "Carta Atenagórica" (The Athenagoric Letter), was a feminist treatise disguised as a religious allegory.

A Controversial Legacy

SOR JUANA'S ADVOCACY for women's rights and her commitment to intellectual pursuits did not come without controversy. Her unapologetic defiance of societal norms led to tensions within the Church and the Inquisition. In 1694, she was forced to renounce her literary and intellectual pursuits and was made to sign a document of self-censorship, effectively silencing her voice.

Legacy and Inspiration

SOR JUANA INÉS DE LA Cruz's life and work continue to inspire scholars, feminists, and advocates for women's rights. Her unwavering dedication to the pursuit of knowledge, her commitment to challenging societal norms, and her fearless expression of her views paved the way for future generations of women to claim their place in academia and society.

Sor Juana's story is a testament to the power of a brilliant mind and the enduring struggle for gender equality. Her legacy serves as a beacon for those who dare to defy societal constraints and push the boundaries of knowledge and freedom. In colonial Mexico, Sor Juana Inés de la Cruz was not just a voice; she was a resounding call for justice, equality, and the liberation of the female intellect.

THESE WOMEN WERE REVOLUTIONARY icons, standing up against oppressive systems, advocating for their rights, and inspiring generations to come. They remind us that change is possible, even when the odds are stacked against us. Their stories of resilience, activism, and advocacy serve as a beacon of hope and a testament to the power of women's voices in shaping the course of history.

As we delve into the lives of these incredible women, we hope their stories will ignite the fire of determination in you, reminding you that the path to equality is paved with the tenacity and courage of those who came before us. Let their stories be a guiding light as we continue our journey through the pages of "Boundless Trailblazers."

Chapter 4: Trailblazers in Science

Welcome to a chapter that celebrates the brilliant minds of women who defied the odds to revolutionize the world of science. In a field where women were often relegated to the shadows of their male counterparts, these remarkable individuals illuminated the path for generations to come. It's a journey through curiosity, resilience, and groundbreaking discoveries.

Marie Curie: The Radiant Pioneer

IN THE ANNALS OF SCIENTIFIC history, few names shine as brightly as Marie Curie. Born Maria Skłodowska in Warsaw, Poland, on November 7, 1867, she would go on to become a pioneer in the fields of physics and chemistry, forever changing our understanding of the world at its most fundamental level.

A Humble Beginning

MARIE CURIE'S JOURNEY to becoming a scientific luminary was marked by hardship and determination. She was the youngest of five children, and her family faced financial struggles, a fact that did not deter her thirst for knowledge. Her early education was disrupted by political unrest in Poland, which was then under Russian control, but she continued to study independently and later, with the help of a secret educational organization that provided classes in science.

In 1891, Maria Skłodowska moved to Paris to continue her education at the Sorbonne. She faced numerous challenges, not least of which was the fact that women were not welcomed with open arms in the male-dominated world of science. Yet, her determination and unwavering belief in the power of education propelled her forward.

A Scientific Partnership and Personal Triumph

AT THE SORBONNE, MARIA met Pierre Curie, a French physicist who would become her husband and life partner. Their collaboration was not only professional but deeply personal, as they embarked on a journey to explore the mysteries of radioactivity together.

The Curies' groundbreaking research led to the discovery of two new elements, polonium and radium, and the development of new theories about atomic structure. They coined the term "radioactivity" itself, forever altering the course of scientific inquiry.

Marie Curie's doctoral thesis on radioactive substances opened the door to her groundbreaking work on the magnetic properties of steel and the discovery of the phenomenon known as radioactivity. In 1903, Marie and Pierre Curie were jointly awarded the Nobel Prize in Physics alongside Henri Becquerel for their pioneering research on radioactivity. This historic recognition marked the first time a woman had ever received a Nobel Prize.

Pioneering the Field of Nuclear Science

MARIE CURIE'S SCIENTIFIC endeavors didn't stop at physics. In 1911, she received her second Nobel Prize, this time in Chemistry, for her work on radium and polonium, further solidifying her place in history. Her research significantly advanced our understanding of the structure of atoms and the nature of radioactivity, laying the foundation for the development of nuclear physics.

Curie's dedication to science was matched by her unwavering commitment to her work. She often handled highly radioactive materials with minimal protection, which unfortunately had long-term health consequences. Tragically, Marie Curie suffered from radiation-related illnesses and passed away on July 4, 1934, but her legacy endures, and her contributions to science remain immeasurable.

A Lasting Legacy

MARIE CURIE'S IMPACT on the world of science extends far beyond her own lifetime. Her pioneering research not only contributed to the development of nuclear physics but also paved the way for important medical advancements, including the use of radiation therapy in cancer treatment.

Her remarkable journey from a young woman struggling against societal norms and financial constraints to becoming the first woman to win a Nobel Prize and the only person to win Nobel Prizes in two different scientific fields is a testament to her indomitable spirit. She not only challenged the norms of her time but continues to inspire generations of women to break barriers and pursue their passions in the world of science.

Marie Curie's story is a reminder that the pursuit of knowledge knows no gender, nationality, or societal constraints. She remains a radiant pioneer, illuminating the path for future scientists, especially women, and demonstrating that with curiosity, dedication, and unwavering belief in oneself, we can achieve the extraordinary.

Ada Lovelace: The Visionary of the Computer Age

ADA LOVELACE, A NAME often regarded as the world's first computer programmer, stands as a remarkable and inspirational figure in the history of technology and science. Born Augusta Ada Byron on December 10, 1815, in London, England, she was the daughter of the famous poet Lord Byron and Annabella Milbanke, a mathematician. Her unique lineage, combining the arts and the sciences, foreshadowed her groundbreaking contributions to the nascent field of computing.

A Mind Blossoms

ADA'S EARLY YEARS WERE marked by a curious and inquisitive mind. Her mother, Lady Byron, was determined to provide Ada with a well-rounded education, particularly in mathematics and science, in an effort to prevent her from inheriting any of the supposed "madness" of her father. Under the guidance of tutors and mentors, Ada quickly developed a keen interest in the sciences.

Her first mentor was Augustus De Morgan, a prominent mathematician and logician, who introduced her to the world of mathematics and formal logic. This education formed the basis of her understanding of computation and, later, her pioneering work in the field.

Collaboration with Charles Babbage

IT WAS THROUGH HER association with Charles Babbage, an inventor and mathematician, that Ada's contributions to computing truly flourished. Babbage had designed a groundbreaking mechanical device called the "Analytical Engine," a forerunner of the modern computer. Ada's understanding of mathematics and her intuitive grasp of Babbage's work led to a profound collaboration between the two.

In 1843, Ada translated an article by Italian mathematician Luigi Federico Menabrea about Babbage's Analytical Engine from French to English. In the process, she added extensive notes, three times longer than the original article, where she not only explained Babbage's machine but also detailed a method for calculating Bernoulli numbers, which are a sequence of rational numbers, using the engine. These notes are often referred to as "Ada's Notes" and are considered to be the world's first computer program.

Visionary Insights

ADA'S CONTRIBUTIONS went beyond mere translation and

computation. In her notes, she elaborated on the potential of Babbage's machine, suggesting that it could manipulate symbols and not just numbers, making it capable of performing any kind of complex calculation. This foresight laid the foundation for the concept of a general-purpose computer, a notion that was far ahead of its time.

Her vision extended even further. She saw that these machines could be used to create music and art, anticipating the creative potential of computers. Her insights into the potential of computing were so profound that she is often hailed as the first person to recognize the full scope and possibilities of computing.

Legacy and Modern Influence

ALTHOUGH THE ANALYTICAL Engine was never built during Ada's lifetime due to financial constraints, her work and vision have left an indelible mark on the field of computer science. The computer programming language "Ada" was named in her honor by the U.S. Department of Defense in the 1970s, emphasizing her continued relevance in the digital age.

Ada Lovelace's legacy serves as an inspiration for future generations of computer scientists, particularly women who have often been underrepresented in the field. Her journey from a young girl with a passion for mathematics to a visionary thinker who laid the foundations of modern computing exemplifies the power of education, curiosity, and imagination.

In the ever-evolving landscape of technology, Ada Lovelace's vision and pioneering spirit continue to guide us. Her story reminds us that great innovations often begin with imagination, collaboration, and the pursuit of knowledge, transcending the boundaries of gender, time, and space. She is, without a doubt, the visionary of the computer age.

Rosalind Franklin: Unveiling the DNA's Mystery

ROSALIND FRANKLIN, a name that should be synonymous with the discovery of the DNA's structure, represents a brilliant but often underappreciated figure in the history of science. Her meticulous work in the mid-20th century played a crucial role in elucidating the mystery of the DNA molecule, a breakthrough that revolutionized our understanding of genetics and laid the foundation for modern molecular biology.

Early Life and Education

ROSALIND FRANKLIN WAS born on July 25, 1920, in London, England, into a family that valued education and intellectual pursuits. She displayed an early aptitude for science, which eventually led her to study chemistry at Newnham College, Cambridge. Her academic excellence was evident from the beginning, and she achieved top honors during her undergraduate studies.

After earning her bachelor's degree, Franklin continued her studies, pursuing a Ph.D. in physical chemistry at Cambridge under the guidance of Ronald Norrish, who would later earn the Nobel Prize in Chemistry. This period marked the beginning of her scientific career, and she quickly established herself as a skilled experimentalist.

Contributions to World War II

DURING WORLD WAR II, Franklin's expertise in physical chemistry was put to practical use. She worked on the development of carbon and coal as adsorbents for gas masks, a project crucial for the war effort. Her contributions not only demonstrated her scientific acumen but also underscored her dedication to applying science to real-world problems.

Pioneering Work on DNA

IT WAS IN THE EARLY 1950s that Rosalind Franklin's career took a fateful turn when she joined King's College London as a research associate. There, she began studying the structure of DNA, a molecule that held the key to the code of life. She employed a technique known as X-ray crystallography, a method to visualize the structure of molecules by analyzing the diffraction patterns of X-rays passing through them.

Franklin's work with DNA fibers and her meticulous X-ray images of DNA molecules were instrumental in elucidating the structure of DNA. Her famous Photograph 51, taken in May 1952, provided a critical piece of evidence that revealed the molecule's double-helix structure. It showcased a distinctive X-shaped pattern, which indicated a helical, or twisted, structure.

The DNA Double Helix Discovery

WHILE ROSALIND FRANKLIN'S work was pivotal in uncovering the DNA's structure, it is important to acknowledge the collaborative nature of science. Her data, particularly Photograph 51, was shown to James Watson and Francis Crick without her knowledge or consent. Their interpretation of her findings, combined with their own research, ultimately led to the famous 1953 Nature paper that proposed the DNA double helix model.

Despite her invaluable contributions, Rosalind Franklin was often marginalized in the history of the DNA discovery. She faced challenges not only from the male-dominated scientific community but also from within her own institution. Her assertiveness and dedication to the integrity of her research often made her a controversial figure, but her commitment to precision and rigor in her work was unwavering.

Legacy and Lasting Impact

TRAGICALLY, ROSALIND Franklin's life was cut short. In 1958, at the age of 37, she passed away from ovarian cancer. Her significant contributions to science have, however, endured and are increasingly recognized. In the decades following her death, she received posthumous acknowledgment for her role in elucidating the structure of DNA.

Rosalind Franklin's work laid the foundation for our understanding of genetics, and her contributions have had a profound impact on the fields of molecular biology and biotechnology. Her story serves as a poignant reminder of the importance of acknowledging the tireless dedication of scientists who, like her, strive to unravel the mysteries of the natural world. Her legacy has become an enduring symbol of scientific rigor and the quest for knowledge, and her work continues to inspire future generations of scientists to boldly venture into the unknown in pursuit of truth.

Modern STEM Pioneers: Breaking Barriers

IN THIS AGE OF RAPID technological advancement, a new generation of modern STEM pioneers has emerged, determined to break down barriers and reshape the world of science, technology, engineering, and mathematics. These women have not only made groundbreaking contributions to their respective fields but have also shattered glass ceilings, inspiring countless others to follow in their footsteps. Here, we explore the stories of some of these remarkable individuals who are pushing the boundaries of what is possible.

Dr. Jane Goodall: Pioneering Primatologist and Conservationist

DR. JANE GOODALL'S groundbreaking work with chimpanzees in the Gombe Stream National Park in Tanzania revolutionized our understanding of primates and reshaped the field of primatology. Armed with little more than her curiosity and a notebook, Goodall made several groundbreaking discoveries. She observed chimpanzees using tools, challenging the belief that tool use was unique to humans. Her research fundamentally altered our perception of the animal kingdom, highlighting the complexity of chimpanzee societies and our connection to them.

But Dr. Goodall's contributions extend beyond science. She has been a tireless advocate for environmental conservation and animal welfare, founding the Jane Goodall Institute and its Roots & Shoots program, which empowers young people to take action in their communities. Her legacy exemplifies the intersection of scientific discovery and environmental activism.

Barbara McClintock: Trailblazing Geneticist

BARBARA MCCLINTOCK, a brilliant geneticist, is celebrated for her pioneering work in maize genetics. Her groundbreaking research on transposons, or "jumping genes," challenged existing paradigms in genetics. In a time when her unconventional ideas faced resistance from the scientific community, McClintock's unwavering dedication to her research led to her being awarded the Nobel Prize in Physiology or Medicine in 1983, making her one of the few women in history to receive the award.

McClintock's work revolutionized our understanding of how genes can move within an organism's genome, impacting fields ranging from agriculture to human genetics. Her story is a testament to the importance of perseverance and the capacity for women to excel in even the most challenging scientific environments.

Dr. Jane Chen: Innovator in Healthcare

DR. JANE CHEN IS A modern pioneer in healthcare technology and innovation. She co-founded Embrace Innovations, a company dedicated to creating affordable and life-saving solutions for premature infants in developing countries. The Embrace Infant Warmer, designed by Dr. Chen and her team, is a low-cost, portable incubator that has saved the lives of thousands of premature babies in resource-constrained areas.

Dr. Chen's work demonstrates that innovation can be a powerful force for good. Her commitment to using technology to address critical healthcare challenges in underserved communities is not only improving infant survival rates but also inspiring the next generation of socially responsible entrepreneurs.

Inspirations Across Generations

THESE MODERN STEM PIONEERS represent a diverse and dynamic group of women who have pushed the boundaries of their fields, each in their unique way. They serve as inspirations for women and girls, demonstrating that gender is not a limitation in the pursuit of scientific and technological excellence.

Their stories underscore the importance of diversity in STEM, as they have shown that a diversity of perspectives leads to innovative breakthroughs. By challenging traditional norms and forging their own paths, these remarkable individuals are paving the way for future generations, encouraging them to dream big and break barriers, while addressing some of the world's most pressing challenges.

As we celebrate these modern STEM pioneers, it is essential to recognize that the journey toward gender equality in STEM is ongoing. Their stories serve as a reminder of the progress made and the work that remains, as women continue to shatter ceilings and redefine what is possible in the world of science,

technology, engineering, and mathematics. They prove that the pursuit of knowledge knows no gender boundaries and that, with determination and a commitment to excellence, anyone can make a profound impact on the world.

In celebrating these extraordinary women, we must also acknowledge the vital importance of mentorship and support networks. The pioneering work of women like Dr. Goodall, Barbara McClintock, and Dr. Chen is not just the product of individual brilliance; it is also a testament to the teachers, mentors, and colleagues who encouraged and believed in them. These relationships are integral in helping aspiring scientists overcome barriers and thrive in their chosen fields.

Furthermore, the stories of these modern STEM pioneers underscore the importance of ensuring access to education, opportunities, and resources for all, regardless of gender or background. By providing a level playing field, we can unleash the full potential of our future innovators and problem solvers.

As we continue to navigate an ever-evolving technological landscape, these women serve as beacons of inspiration, demonstrating that the frontiers of knowledge remain open to exploration by anyone willing to embark on the journey. Their pioneering spirit, tenacity, and innovative thinking are not only changing the face of science but also shaping a more inclusive and equitable future for all. These modern STEM pioneers are not just breaking barriers; they are building bridges for the generations that follow, fostering a world where the marvels of science and technology are accessible to all, regardless of their gender or background.

IN THE PAGES OF THIS chapter, we've encountered women who boldly ventured into uncharted scientific territories, making history and reshaping the future. Their stories serve as a powerful reminder that passion, determination, and an unyielding thirst for knowledge can break down even the most formidable barriers.

Stay tuned as we continue our exploration of incredible women who have shaped the course of history, and find out how their stories can ignite the trailblazer within you.

Chapter 5: Women in Sports

Picture this: a world where women were not just allowed to compete in sports, but excelled beyond anyone's wildest expectations. A world where female athletes broke records, shattered glass ceilings, and captivated audiences with their sheer determination and unmatched talent. Welcome to the inspiring universe of women in sports, where grit, passion, and relentless dedication redefine the game.

In this chapter, we explore the triumphs, struggles, and remarkable stories of female athletes who paved the way for future generations. These women defied societal norms, challenged stereotypes, and showed the world that gender is no barrier to greatness.

Wilma Rudolph: The Fastest Woman in the World

WILMA RUDOLPH'S STORY is one of remarkable perseverance, determination, and sheer athletic excellence. Born prematurely on June 23, 1940, in Saint Bethlehem, Tennessee, she faced considerable adversity from her very first days. At the age of four, she was diagnosed with polio, a disease that left her with a twisted left leg and the prospect of never walking again. However, Wilma's spirit and her family's unwavering support would prove that no obstacle was too great for her to overcome.

Wilma was the 20th of 22 siblings, and her family's support was instrumental in her recovery. Her mother, Blanche, was a constant pillar of strength, helping Wilma through grueling leg exercises and taking her to weekly therapy sessions, which were often distant from their home. Wilma's parents' belief in her potential was unshakable, and it instilled in her the determination to conquer her physical limitations.

Through years of diligent work, Wilma gradually regained her ability to walk. By the time she was twelve, she had not only regained her mobility but had also developed an interest in basketball. Little did anyone know that this would be the beginning of her remarkable journey as an athlete.

Her basketball skills were evident, and she soon became a star player at her high school, becoming known for her speed and agility on the court. Her exceptional talent caught the eye of Ed Temple, the renowned coach of the Tennessee State University Tigerbelles, a track and field team.

Under Temple's guidance, Wilma began her transformation from a talented basketball player to a track and field sensation. The world would soon come to know her as "The Tornado" due to her incredible speed. Her dedication to training was unwavering, and she worked tirelessly to fine-tune her athletic abilities.

In 1956, at the Melbourne Olympics, Wilma made her first appearance on the international stage. Although she didn't win a medal, her determination to compete at the highest level of track and field was evident. However, her most defining moment would come at the 1960 Rome Olympics.

The 1960 Olympics were a turning point for women in sports. It was here that Wilma Rudolph made history and became a symbol of female athletic excellence. She competed in the 100m, 200m, and 4x100m relay events, winning gold in each one. These triumphs made her the first American woman to achieve such a feat in a single Olympics. Her blazing speed in the 100m and 200m races earned her the nickname "The Fastest Woman in the World."

Wilma Rudolph's victories were not just personal achievements;

they were a testament to the strength of the human spirit and the power of perseverance. Her remarkable success was a source of inspiration for women and athletes worldwide. She had not only broken records but also shattered the notion that women couldn't compete at the highest levels of sports.

After her historic Olympic victories, Wilma Rudolph continued to inspire by using her platform to advocate for civil rights and equal opportunities for athletes of all backgrounds. She believed in the power of sports to transcend boundaries and bring people together, and she used her influence to support that cause.

Wilma's legacy endures as an enduring symbol of triumph over adversity and a reminder that with determination and unwavering dedication, one can achieve greatness in the face of seemingly insurmountable odds. Her story is a testament to the indomitable spirit of human beings and a source of inspiration for generations to come, reminding us that "impossible" is just another word for "I'm possible."

Serena Williams: A Tennis Icon

WHEN YOU THINK OF TENNIS, one name stands out above all others, Serena Williams. Her incredible journey from the streets of Compton, California, to becoming one of the most dominant and iconic athletes in the history of the sport is nothing short of awe-inspiring. Serena's career has been marked by unparalleled skill, unyielding determination, and a profound impact that extends far beyond the tennis court.

A Humble Beginning

SERENA JAMEKA WILLIAMS was born on September 26, 1981, in Saginaw, Michigan, but her family relocated to Compton, a city known for its high crime rates. Raised by her father, Richard Williams, and her mother, Oracene Price, Serena grew up alongside her older sister

Venus, who would also become a tennis superstar. The family's humble beginnings had a profound influence on Serena's outlook on life and her approach to tennis.

Serena's journey in tennis began at the age of three, when her father introduced her to the sport. Richard Williams, who had no previous experience with tennis, studied instructional videos and books to teach his daughters the fundamentals of the game. This early tutelage not only cultivated Serena's tennis skills but also instilled in her a strong work ethic and a fighting spirit.

A Trailblazing Career

SERENA WILLIAMS TURNED professional in 1995, and from that moment on, her ascent in the tennis world was nothing short of meteoric. Known for her powerful serve, unmatched athleticism, and mental toughness, Serena quickly became a force to be reckoned with on the court.

Serena's first Grand Slam victory came at the 1999 US Open, where she defeated Martina Hingis in the final. This win marked the beginning of a remarkable Grand Slam-winning career. She has now won 23 Grand Slam singles titles, the most by any player in the Open Era, and just one shy of the all-time record held by Margaret Court.

Her dominance on the tennis court is unparalleled. Serena has held the World No. 1 ranking multiple times and has won titles on all surfaces, showcasing her adaptability and versatility as a player. Her relentless pursuit of excellence and her ability to maintain peak performance over two decades are a testament to her dedication and unwavering passion for the sport.

Breaking Barriers

SERENA WILLIAMS IS not only celebrated for her tennis achievements but also for her pioneering efforts in breaking down barriers. Throughout her career, she has been an advocate for gender equality in sports. Her outspoken stance on equal pay for female athletes has had a profound impact on the tennis world and sports in general. Her efforts have helped narrow the pay gap between male and female players, setting a powerful example for athletes in all disciplines.

Overcoming Adversity

SERENA'S CAREER HAS been punctuated by numerous highs, but it has also been marked by significant challenges and adversity. She faced serious injuries and health issues, including a life-threatening pulmonary embolism, which threatened to end her career. Yet, her remarkable resilience and determination saw her come back stronger each time.

Legacy and Inspiration

SERENA WILLIAMS IS more than a tennis legend; she is a global icon who has transcended the world of sports. Her impact on the game, on women's rights, and on the perception of female athletes is immeasurable. Her journey from Compton to the pinnacle of tennis success has inspired countless individuals worldwide to chase their dreams, no matter their background.

Serena's story is a testament to the boundless potential that resides within every individual. It illustrates the power of determination, hard work, and an unwavering belief in oneself. Her legacy will continue to motivate generations of athletes and non-athletes alike, reminding us that anything is possible when you dare to dream, work relentlessly, and embrace the challenges along the way. Serena Williams is not just a tennis icon; she is a symbol of resilience, empowerment, and a living testament to the idea that, in life, the sky is the limit.

Billie Jean King: A Champion of Equality

BILLIE JEAN KING IS a tennis legend whose impact on the sport extends far beyond her numerous titles and championships. She is renowned for her relentless pursuit of gender equality, not just in tennis but in all aspects of life. Billie Jean King's journey from a young tennis prodigy to an iconic advocate for social change is a testament to her unwavering commitment to justice, fairness, and equal rights.

Early Life and Tennis Stardom

BILLIE JEAN MOFFITT, later known as Billie Jean King, was born on November 22, 1943, in Long Beach, California. She exhibited an early talent for tennis, and by the age of 11, she was already winning tournaments. Billie Jean's determination and love for the sport led her to the pinnacle of tennis, and in 1966, she was ranked as the No. 1 female player in the world.

Her skills on the court were evident in her many accomplishments, including winning 39 Grand Slam titles in singles, doubles, and mixed doubles. Her aggressive and competitive style of play, along with her pioneering use of the two-handed backhand, made her a formidable opponent. Her most iconic victories included the famous "Battle of the Sexes" match against Bobby Riggs in 1973, which she won, solidifying her reputation as a tennis icon.

Equal Pay for Equal Play

ONE OF THE MOST SIGNIFICANT contributions Billie Jean King made to the world of sports was her tireless advocacy for equal pay. In 1970, she, along with eight other female tennis players, signed a $1 contract with World Tennis magazine, highlighting the vast disparity in prize money between male and female tennis players. Their protest was the catalyst for change, leading to a more equitable distribution of prize money.

Billie Jean King's efforts went beyond tennis. She saw the fight for equal pay as a part of the broader struggle for gender equality, and her commitment to the cause remains an enduring legacy. Her advocacy laid the groundwork for women's rights in sports, helping pave the way for equal pay in other fields.

The Battle of the Sexes

PERHAPS BILLIE JEAN King's most iconic moment was the "Battle of the Sexes" match against Bobby Riggs in 1973. The world watched in anticipation as Billie Jean King, the reigning Wimbledon champion, faced the former men's World No. 1, Bobby Riggs. The match transcended the realm of sports, becoming a symbol of the feminist movement and a testament to a woman's capability to compete at the highest level.

Billie Jean King's victory in the match was not just about tennis; it was a declaration that women could excel in any arena, challenging stereotypes and breaking down gender barriers. Her win was a defining moment in the history of women in sports and the fight for gender equality.

Advocacy and Leadership

BILLIE JEAN KING'S contributions to equality extended beyond the tennis court. She co-founded the Women's Tennis Association (WTA) and played a pivotal role in establishing the Women's Sports Foundation, organizations dedicated to advancing opportunities for women in sports.

Throughout her life, she continued to be a vocal advocate for gender equality and LGBTQ+ rights. Her advocacy remains a testament to the power of using one's platform for change. She tirelessly fought for equality, proving that sports can be a vehicle for social progress.

Legacy and Inspiration

BILLIE JEAN KING'S legacy is one of strength, determination, and unwavering commitment to justice. Her impact on gender equality in sports has had a profound influence on the landscape of women's athletics. She remains an inspiration to athletes, activists, and anyone seeking to challenge societal norms and create a more equitable world.

Billie Jean King's story is a testament to the enduring power of sports as a catalyst for social change. Her pioneering efforts continue to inspire generations of athletes and advocates, reminding us that the pursuit of equality is a journey worth taking, no matter the obstacles or adversity encountered along the way. She is not just a champion in tennis; she is a champion of equality and justice for all.

Simone Biles: Defying Gravity

OUR CHAPTER WOULDN'T be complete without celebrating modern athletes like Simone Biles. Hailing from the world of gymnastics, Simone has taken the sport to new heights with her extraordinary skills and unmatched athleticism. She's redefined what's possible, pushing the boundaries of what a gymnast can achieve.

Simone's story is one of hard work, dedication, and breaking stereotypes about body image in sports. She's shown that excellence in gymnastics knows no boundaries, and her fearless pursuit of perfection has earned her a special place in the hearts of fans worldwide.

Simone Biles is a name synonymous with gymnastics excellence. Her journey from a young, talented gymnast to a global superstar is a story of determination, strength, and the relentless pursuit of perfection. Simone's impact on gymnastics and her ability to defy gravity, both literally and figuratively, have made her one of the most celebrated athletes of our time.

Early Life and Introduction to Gymnastics

BORN ON MARCH 14, 1997, in Columbus, Ohio, Simone Arianne Biles had a challenging childhood. She and her three siblings were placed in foster care due to her mother's struggles with addiction. Eventually, Simone was adopted by her maternal grandparents, Nellie and Ron Biles, who provided her with a stable and loving home.

Simone's introduction to gymnastics was a twist of fate. At the age of six, she accompanied a daycare field trip to a local gymnastics center. Her raw talent and fearlessness on the apparatuses caught the eye of the coach, Aimee Boorman. Aimee recognized Simone's potential and invited her to join the gym's training program.

Rise to Stardom

FROM THAT MOMENT, SIMONE'S life changed forever. She quickly rose through the ranks of junior gymnastics and, by the age of 16, had become a dominant force in the world of gymnastics. Her explosive power, unparalleled athleticism, and innovative skills set her apart from her peers.

Simone's first major victory came at the 2013 World Championships, where she won the all-around title. This marked the beginning of her reign as one of the most exceptional gymnasts in the world. Her signature moves, including the "Biles" on floor exercise and the "Biles II" on balance beam, pushed the boundaries of the sport and earned her global recognition.

2016 Rio Olympics: Making History

THE 2016 RIO OLYMPICS were a defining moment for Simone Biles. She entered the competition as the favorite and lived up to the expectations by winning four gold medals in the all-around, team, vault, and floor exercise. She also claimed a bronze medal on the balance beam. Her dynamic routines, precision, and seemingly effortless flips left both fans and fellow gymnasts in awe.

What makes Simone's achievements all the more remarkable is that she defied traditional norms of gymnastics. Standing at 4 feet 8 inches, she is smaller than many of her competitors, yet her remarkable strength and power allowed her to perform gravity-defying flips and twists with unrivaled precision. Her unprecedented skills and athleticism demonstrated that excellence in gymnastics knows no bounds.

Overcoming Adversity

BEHIND THE SCENES, Simone faced significant challenges, including the revelation of sexual abuse within the USA Gymnastics organization. She and her fellow survivors came forward to shed light on the abuse and advocate for justice and accountability. Simone's resilience and courage in the face of these difficult circumstances earned her not only admiration as an athlete but also as an advocate for change.

Tokyo 2020 and Beyond

IN THE LEAD-UP TO THE Tokyo 2020 Olympics (held in 2021 due to the pandemic), Simone faced unprecedented pressure and expectations. Despite these challenges, she showcased her extraordinary abilities and earned herself several more medals, including a silver in the team competition, a bronze in the balance beam, and a bronze in the individual all-around. She proved that even the most accomplished athletes can face mental health struggles and need support.

Simone Biles has consistently used her platform to promote mental health awareness, emphasizing the importance of self-care and well-being. Her openness about her struggles has not only inspired fellow athletes but has also helped destigmatize discussions surrounding mental health in sports.

Legacy and Inspiration

SIMONE BILES'S STORY is a testament to the indomitable spirit of human beings and the boundless potential that resides within each of us. Her ability to defy gravity on the gymnastics floor is a physical manifestation of her unyielding determination and the embodiment of a dream realized.

Simone Biles is more than a gymnast; she is an inspiration to athletes of all disciplines and an advocate for mental health awareness. Her journey from foster care to Olympic stardom is a remarkable narrative of triumph over adversity, resilience, and the relentless pursuit of perfection. She has redefined what is possible in gymnastics, and her impact on the sport and the world reaches far beyond the apparatuses and medals. Simone Biles is a living example that no obstacle is too high to overcome and that the sky is not the limit; it's just the starting point for those who dare to dream and defy gravity.

THESE WOMEN IN SPORTS, along with countless others, have shown that talent, dedication, and passion have no gender. They've blazed a trail for future generations of female athletes, proving that in the arena, on the field, or in the gym, women can excel beyond imagination. They've not only rewritten the record books but also rewritten the rules. Their stories continue to inspire, reminding us that with unwavering determination, we can conquer any challenge, break any barrier, and achieve greatness.

As you delve into their stories, remember that these women in sports are not just athletes; they are pioneers who've paved the way for a more inclusive and equal world. Their stories are a testament to the boundless potential that exists within all of us. So, let their journeys inspire you to chase your dreams and redefine what's possible in your own life.

Chapter 6: Icons of Literature

In the hushed corners of libraries and amidst the crisp pages of well-loved books, the voices of extraordinary women echoed through the annals of literary history. These women, the unsung heroines of the written word, crafted worlds with their pens and ignited the imaginations of generations. Let us embark on a journey through the pages of time, exploring the lives and works of these literary luminaries.

Jane Austen: A Pen Mightier Than a Sword

IN THE ROLLING HILLS of England, Jane Austen penned stories that transcended eras. With wit as sharp as the quill she wrote with, Austen introduced readers to strong-willed heroines navigating societal norms. Elizabeth Bennet, Emma Woodhouse, and Elinor Dashwood stood as beacons of independence, challenging the constraints imposed upon women in the early 19th century. Through works like "Pride and Prejudice" and "Sense and Sensibility," Austen didn't just write novels; she penned social commentaries that continue to resonate today.

In the serene, bucolic setting of early 19th-century England, where societal norms dictated the path women should tread, Jane Austen emerged as a literary luminary. Her impact on the world of literature and her profound influence on the way we perceive the female experience are nothing short of extraordinary.

Born in 1775 in the picturesque village of Steventon in Hampshire, England, Jane Austen was the seventh of eight children in a close-knit family. Her father, a clergyman, provided her with access to his extensive library, where young Jane discovered the transformative power of books and the written word. This early exposure to literature ignited a passion that would shape her destiny.

Austen's novels serve as a unique window into the society of her time, offering readers a glimpse of the intricate web of social conventions, class hierarchies, and gender expectations that defined the Regency era. Her writing was characterized by a keen wit, incisive observations, and a profound understanding of human nature. Through her novels, she navigated the complex nuances of relationships, love, and the constraints placed on women.

At the heart of Austen's literary canon is the indomitable spirit of her heroines. From Elizabeth Bennet's unyielding independence in "Pride and Prejudice" to Emma Woodhouse's spirited matchmaking in "Emma," her female characters defied the passivity society expected of them. These women were not content to merely accept their fates but actively sought to shape their own destinies, challenging the status quo of the time.

Austen's exploration of themes such as marriage, money, and manners was not confined to mere romance; it was a societal commentary that highlighted the absurdity and hypocrisy of the society in which she lived. Her razor-sharp irony and satire exposed the shortcomings of the aristocracy, and her subtle critiques encouraged readers to question the prevailing norms.

"Jane Eyre" author Charlotte Brontë once remarked, "The passions are perfectly unknown to [Austen]; she rejects even a speaking acquaintance with that stormy sisterhood." While Brontë's words reflected the prevalent sentiment of her time, they also underscored the subtlety of Austen's approach. Beneath the genteel exterior of her novels, Austen's characters experienced deep and genuine emotions, expressing them with an authenticity that transcends the ages. Austen's characters may not have wielded swords or led revolutions, but they fought their battles with words, wit, and resilience.

Jane Austen's works, including "Sense and Sensibility," "Mansfield Park," and "Northanger Abbey," have resonated across centuries and continents, adapting to different cultures and languages. Her legacy endures not only in her novels but also in numerous film and television adaptations that introduce her timeless narratives to new generations.

Jane Austen, often described as the "inventor of the domestic novel," possessed a profound ability to breathe life into her characters and craft stories that continue to captivate readers. Her novels are more than just classics; they are guideposts for the journey of women seeking self-determination and autonomy in a world that seeks to define them. In her own way, Jane Austen was a trailblazer, and her pen was indeed mightier than a sword, carving a path for future generations of female writers and proving that the power of the written word knows no gender, era, or societal constraint.

Virginia Woolf: Waves of Feminist Literature

IN THE EARLY 20TH CENTURY, amidst the shifting tides of societal expectations, Virginia Woolf emerged as a trailblazer. With her experimental prose and deep introspection, Woolf shattered literary conventions. Her seminal work, "Mrs. Dalloway," delved into the complexities of the human mind, challenging traditional narrative structures. Woolf's pioneering feminist essays, including "A Room of One's Own," advocated for women's intellectual freedom and paved the way for future generations of female writers.

Virginia Woolf, the iconic English writer of the early 20th century, left an indelible mark on the world of literature. Her innovative and groundbreaking works not only redefined the narrative structure but also propelled the feminist movement into uncharted waters. Woolf's life and writings remain a testament to her profound intellectual contributions and her pivotal role in shaping modernist literature and feminist discourse.

Born in London in 1882, Virginia Woolf was part of the influential

Bloomsbury Group, a collective of writers, artists, and thinkers who challenged the societal norms of their time. Her privileged upbringing provided her with access to education and intellectual pursuits, laying the foundation for her remarkable career as a writer and thinker.

Woolf's literary journey began with her early novels, "The Voyage Out" and "Night and Day." However, it was with her third novel, "Jacob's Room," that she truly began to experiment with narrative form, foreshadowing the innovative techniques she would later employ in her more renowned works.

It was Woolf's fourth novel, "Mrs. Dalloway," published in 1925, that marked a turning point in her career and modernist literature as a whole. The novel unfolds over a single day, offering readers a profound insight into the minds of its characters. With her stream-of-consciousness narrative style, Woolf delved into the inner thoughts and emotions of her characters, defying conventional storytelling. In doing so, she revealed the complex inner lives of her female characters, particularly Clarissa Dalloway, and emphasized their struggles with societal expectations.

Woolf's groundbreaking essay, "A Room of One's Own," published in 1929, remains a cornerstone of feminist literature. In this essay, she argued that women's economic independence and a space of their own were essential for creative expression. Woolf used her own experiences as a female writer to highlight the historical disparities in opportunities and recognition between male and female authors. She called for a feminist literary tradition that would give women the freedom to write their own stories, unencumbered by the expectations of a male-dominated society.

With her magnum opus, "To the Lighthouse," published in 1927, Woolf continued to push the boundaries of narrative structure and deepened her exploration of the female experience. The novel's introspective narrative journey through the Ramsay family's lives offers an intricate portrayal of the complexities of female relationships, the passage of time, and the role of memory in shaping our lives. The novel, often considered one of her greatest works, showcased her remarkable ability to capture the essence of human consciousness.

Woolf's legacy as a feminist writer is further solidified by her novels "Orlando" and "The Waves." "Orlando," published in 1928, is a remarkable gender-fluid narrative that spans four centuries, exploring themes of identity, sexuality, and time. "The Waves," published in 1931, employs a poetic prose style to weave the interconnected stories of six characters, emphasizing the fluidity of identity and the influence of relationships on personal development.

Virginia Woolf's work transcended the literary realm to become a powerful voice in the feminist movement. Her novels and essays, coupled with her own lived experiences and advocacy for women's rights, have inspired generations of women to seek independence and creative expression. She illuminated the intricate and nuanced interior lives of women in a world that had often relegated them to the periphery of literature.

Tragically, Woolf's life was marred by mental health struggles, culminating in her suicide in 1941. Nevertheless, her literary legacy continues to thrive, and her contributions to feminist literature remain an enduring source of inspiration and a testament to the power of the written word to challenge societal norms, reshape narratives, and create waves of change in the pursuit of gender equality. Virginia Woolf, a literary pioneer, remains a symbol of strength and resilience in the face of adversity, her waves of feminist literature rippling through the generations.

Maya Angelou: Poetry as a Conduit for the Soul

MAYA ANGELOU, A PHENOMENAL woman, etched her name into the annals of literary history through her poignant poetry and mesmerizing memoirs. With verses that soared like the caged bird she wrote about, Angelou explored themes of identity, race, and resilience. Her autobiographical masterpiece, "I Know Why the Caged Bird Sings," became a beacon of hope for countless readers, encouraging them to embrace their own stories, no matter how challenging the circumstances.

Maya Angelou, the renowned American author, poet, and civil rights activist, carved a distinctive place for herself in the annals of literature and social justice. Her life was a testament to the power of resilience, and her poetry served as a profound conduit for the human soul, carrying messages of hope, strength, and transformation.

Maya Angelou's life was marked by early challenges that could have easily stifled her spirit. Born Marguerite Annie Johnson on April 4, 1928, in St. Louis, Missouri, she faced hardships that included racial discrimination, sexual abuse, and poverty. However, these early trials became the crucible in which her indomitable spirit was forged. Her journey from a silenced and traumatized child to a celebrated writer and poet is a story of remarkable transformation.

It was during a period of silence and self-imposed muteness in her youth, after a traumatic incident, that Angelou first discovered her love for literature. She devoured books, absorbing the words and worlds within them. Literature became her sanctuary, a place where her soul found solace and voice. This love for words and stories laid the foundation for her future as a poet and writer.

Angelou's life was a tapestry woven with numerous experiences, ranging from her work as a calypso dancer and nightclub performer to her involvement in the civil rights movement. It was these diverse experiences that lent her a unique perspective and a wealth of material to draw upon in her writings.

Her first memoir, "I Know Why the Caged Bird Sings," published in 1969, was a groundbreaking work that resonated with readers around the world. The title, a reference to a line from the poem

"Sympathy" by Paul Laurence Dunbar, captured the essence of her own life and the experiences of many marginalized individuals. In her memoir, Angelou explored themes of race, identity, and womanhood, revealing the triumph of the human spirit in the face of adversity.

Maya Angelou's poetry, characterized by its vivid imagery and rhythmic flow, explored the universal human experiences of love, pain, and resilience. Her collection "And Still I Rise," published in 1978, remains a classic in American literature. The titular poem, "Still I Rise," is an anthem of empowerment, defiance, and unbreakable spirit. It celebrates the resilience of the human soul, asserting that no matter the obstacles and prejudices faced, one can rise above them.

"Phenomenal Woman" is another of Angelou's iconic poems. It exudes a sense of self-assuredness and self-worth that has empowered women to embrace their uniqueness and beauty. Through her words, Angelou championed the idea that inner strength and confidence could defy societal norms and expectations.

Her poem "On the Pulse of Morning," which she recited at the inauguration of President Bill Clinton in 1993, encapsulated her ability to bridge the personal and the political. In this poem, Angelou urged humanity to come together, to recognize the shared responsibility of creating a just and compassionate society. Her words transcended politics, echoing a call for unity, empathy, and social justice.

Maya Angelou's legacy is not only in her literary contributions but also in her role as a civil rights activist. She worked alongside figures like Malcolm X and Dr. Martin Luther King Jr., lending her voice to the battle for civil rights, justice, and equality. Her ability to engage with both the personal and the public, to combine the profound and the poetic, marked her as a true Renaissance woman.

Maya Angelou's life and work inspire generations to embrace their individuality, rise above adversity, and use the power of words to convey the depths of the human experience. Her poetry serves as a timeless conduit for the soul, transmitting messages of hope, resilience, and transformation to all who encounter it. In her words, she continues to remind us that we are all caged birds, but within us lies the strength to rise, to sing, and to soar. Maya Angelou, a poet of the soul, will forever be remembered for her extraordinary ability to unite hearts and minds through the art of poetry.

Charlotte Brontë: The Brontës' Literary Legacy

IN THE HEART OF THE rugged Yorkshire moors during the 19th century, the Brontë sisters—Charlotte, Emily, and Anne—etched their names in the annals of literary history. Of the three, Charlotte Brontë stood as a remarkable figure whose contributions to literature continue to captivate and inspire readers worldwide. Her life and work, deeply rooted in the Victorian era, created a literary legacy that transcends time and place.

Early Life and Family

BORN ON APRIL 21, 1816, in Thornton, Yorkshire, England, Charlotte Brontë was the eldest of six siblings. Her father, Patrick Brontë, was a clergyman, and her mother, Maria Brontë, died when Charlotte was just five years old. Her early years were marked by the loss of her mother and two older sisters, Maria and Elizabeth, to tuberculosis. These early experiences of loss and grief would cast a shadow over her life and profoundly influence her writing.

As children, Charlotte and her siblings, including Emily and Anne, embarked on imaginative adventures in a world of make-believe, creating fictional worlds and characters that would later find their way into their novels. Their tiny, secluded parsonage in Haworth became the backdrop for these imaginative escapades, ultimately forming the backdrop for their literary endeavors.

The Novels

CHARLOTTE BRONTË IS best known for her novels, particularly "Jane Eyre," published in 1847 under the pseudonym "Currer Bell." "Jane Eyre" is a story of a young orphaned governess who faces daunting trials and tribulations but remains unyielding in her quest for love, independence, and self-respect. The character of Jane is celebrated for her spiritedness, strong moral compass, and the assertion of her individuality—a remarkable portrayal of a woman's strength in a time when societal expectations were particularly constraining.

The novel's enigmatic and brooding hero, Mr. Rochester, added a complex dimension to the narrative, making "Jane Eyre" a timeless classic that continues to resonate with readers. Brontë's exploration of themes such as class, gender, and love in the novel demonstrated her deep insight into the human psyche and her ability to create complex, authentic characters.

In "Shirley" (1849) and "Villette" (1853), Brontë delved into themes of feminism, love, and societal expectations, bringing to life strong, independent female protagonists who navigated the turbulent waters of 19th-century England. Her heroines, like Caroline Helstone in "Shirley" and Lucy Snowe in "Villette," defied traditional feminine roles and sought to chart their own destinies.

"Jane Eyre" by Charlotte Brontë contains several empowering moments and chapters that resonate with women seeking independence and self-worth. One of the most empowering chapters is in Volume 3, Chapter 1, when Jane confronts Mr. Rochester about her feelings and her desire for an equal partnership. In this chapter, Jane asserts her independence and refuses to be marginalized or controlled. Here's an excerpt from that chapter:

"I am no bird; and no net ensnares me: I am a free human being with an independent will, which I now exert to leave you."

In this chapter, Jane refuses to be subjected to societal norms or the limitations imposed on her as a woman. She stands up for herself and her beliefs, ultimately choosing self-respect and independence over a love that would compromise her integrity. This moment is particularly empowering as it underscores the importance of self-worth and personal agency for women, even in the face of societal pressures and expectations.

Chapter 1 of Jane Eyre

There was no possibility of taking a walk that day. We had been wandering, indeed, in the leafless shrubbery an hour in the morning; but since dinner (Mrs. Reed, when there was no company, dined early) the cold winter wind had brought with it clouds so sombre, and a rain so penetrating, that further out-door exercise was now out of the question.

I was glad of it: I never liked long walks, especially on chilly afternoons: dreadful to me was the coming home in the raw twilight, with nipped fingers and toes, and a heart saddened by the chidings of Bessie, the nurse, and humbled by the consciousness of my physical inferiority to Eliza, John, and Georgiana Reed.

The said Eliza, John, and Georgiana were now clustered round their mama in the drawing-room: she lay reclined on a sofa by the fireside, and with her darlings about her (for the time neither quarrelling nor crying) looked perfectly happy. Me, she had dispensed from joining the group; saying, "She regretted to be under the necessity of keeping me at a distance; but that until she heard from Bessie, and could discover by her own observation, that I was endeavouring in good earnest to acquire a more sociable and childlike disposition, a more attractive and sprightly manner—something lighter, franker, more natural, as it were—she really must exclude me from privileges intended only for contented, happy, little children."

"What does Bessie say I have done?" I asked.

"Jane, I don't like cavillers or questioners; besides, there is something truly forbidding in a child taking up her elders in that manner. Be seated somewhere; and until you can speak pleasantly, remain silent."

A breakfast-room adjoined the drawing-room, I slipped in there. It contained a bookcase: I soon possessed myself of a volume, taking care that it should be one stored with pictures. I mounted into the window-seat: gathering up my feet, I sat cross-legged, like a Turk; and, having drawn the red moreen curtain nearly close, I was shrined in double retirement.

Folds of scarlet drapery shut in my view to the right hand; to the left were the clear panes of glass, protecting, but not separating me from the drear November day. At intervals, while turning over the leaves of my book, I studied the aspect of that winter afternoon. Afar, it offered a pale blank of mist and cloud; near a scene of wet lawn and storm-beat shrub, with ceaseless rain sweeping away wildly before a long and lamentable blast.

I returned to my book—Bewick's History of British Birds: the letterpress thereof I cared little for, generally speaking; and yet there were certain introductory pages that, child as I was, I could not pass quite as a blank. They were those which treat of the haunts of sea-fowl; of "the solitary rocks and promontories" by them only inhabited; of the coast of Norway, studded with isles from its southern extremity, the Lindeness, or Naze, to the North Cape—

"Where the Northern Ocean, in vast whirls,
Boils round the naked, melancholy isles
Of farthest Thule; and the Atlantic surge
Pours in among the stormy Hebrides."

Nor could I pass unnoticed the suggestion of the bleak shores of Lapland, Siberia, Spitzbergen, Nova Zembla, Iceland, Greenland, with "the vast sweep of the Arctic Zone, and those forlorn regions of dreary space,—that reservoir of frost and snow, where firm fields of ice, the accumulation of centuries of winters, glazed in Alpine heights above heights, surround the pole, and concentre the multiplied rigours of extreme cold." Of these death-white realms I formed an idea of my own: shadowy, like all the half-comprehended notions that float dim through children's brains, but strangely impressive. The words in these introductory pages connected themselves with the succeeding vignettes, and gave significance to the rock standing up alone in a sea of billow and spray; to the broken boat stranded on a desolate coast; to the cold and ghastly moon glancing through bars of cloud at a wreck just sinking.

I cannot tell what sentiment haunted the quite solitary churchyard, with its inscribed headstone; its gate, its two trees, its low horizon, girdled by a broken wall, and its newly-risen crescent, attesting the hour of eventide.

The two ships becalmed on a torpid sea, I believed to be marine phantoms.

The fiend pinning down the thief's pack behind him, I passed over quickly: it was an object of terror.

So was the black horned thing seated aloof on a rock, surveying a distant crowd surrounding a gallows.

Each picture told a story; mysterious often to my undeveloped understanding and imperfect feelings, yet ever profoundly interesting: as interesting as the tales Bessie sometimes narrated on winter evenings, when she chanced to be in good humour; and when, having brought her ironing-table to the nursery hearth, she allowed us to sit about it, and while she got up Mrs. Reed's lace frills, and crimped her nightcap borders, fed our eager attention with passages of love and adventure taken from old fairy tales and other ballads; or (as at a later period I discovered) from the pages of Pamela, and Henry, Earl of Moreland.

With Bewick on my knee, I was then happy: happy at least in my way. I feared nothing but interruption, and that came too soon. The breakfast-room door opened.

"Boh! Madam Mope!" cried the voice of John Reed; then he paused: he found the room apparently empty.

"Where the dickens is she!" he continued. "Lizzy! Georgy! (calling to his sisters) Joan is not here: tell mama she is run out into the rain—bad animal!"

"It is well I drew the curtain," thought I; and I wished fervently he might not discover my hiding-place: nor would John Reed have found it

out himself; he was not quick either of vision or conception; but Eliza just put her head in at the door, and said at once—

"She is in the window-seat, to be sure, Jack."

And I came out immediately, for I trembled at the idea of being dragged forth by the said Jack.

"What do you want?" I asked, with awkward diffidence.

"Say, 'What do you want, Master Reed?'" was the answer. "I want you to come here;" and seating himself in an arm-chair, he intimated by a gesture that I was to approach and stand before him.

John Reed was a schoolboy of fourteen years old; four years older than I, for I was but ten: large and stout for his age, with a dingy and unwholesome skin; thick lineaments in a spacious visage, heavy limbs and large extremities. He gorged himself habitually at table, which made him bilious, and gave him a dim and bleared eye and flabby cheeks. He ought now to have been at school; but his mama had taken him home for a month or two, "on account of his delicate health." Mr. Miles, the master, affirmed that he would do very well if he had fewer cakes and sweetmeats sent him from home; but the mother's heart turned from an opinion so harsh, and inclined rather to the more refined idea that John's sallowness was owing to over-application and, perhaps, to pining after home.

John had not much affection for his mother and sisters, and an antipathy to me. He bullied and punished me; not two or three times in the week, nor once or twice in the day, but continually: every nerve I had feared him, and every morsel of flesh in my bones shrank when he came near. There were moments when I was bewildered by the terror he inspired, because I had no appeal whatever against either his menaces or his inflictions; the servants did not like to offend their young master by taking my part against him, and Mrs. Reed was blind and deaf on the subject: she never saw him strike or heard him abuse me, though he did both now and then in her very presence, more frequently, however, behind her back.

Habitually obedient to John, I came up to his chair: he spent some three minutes in thrusting out his tongue at me as far as he could without damaging the roots: I knew he would soon strike, and while dreading the blow, I mused on the disgusting and ugly appearance of him who would presently deal it. I wonder if he read that notion in my face; for, all at once, without speaking, he struck suddenly and strongly. I tottered, and on regaining my equilibrium retired back a step or two from his chair.

"That is for your impudence in answering mama awhile since," said he, "and for your sneaking way of getting behind curtains, and for the look you had in your eyes two minutes since, you rat!"

Accustomed to John Reed's abuse, I never had an idea of replying to it; my care was how to endure the blow which would certainly follow the insult.

"What were you doing behind the curtain?" he asked.

"I was reading."

"Show the book."

I returned to the window and fetched it thence.

"You have no business to take our books; you are a dependent, mama says; you have no money; your father left you none; you ought to beg, and not to live here with gentlemen's children like us, and eat the same meals we do, and wear clothes at our mama's expense. Now, I'll teach you to rummage my bookshelves: for they are mine; all the house belongs to me, or will do in a few years. Go and stand by the door, out of the way of the mirror and the windows."

I did so, not at first aware what was his intention; but when I saw him lift and poise the book and stand in act to hurl it, I instinctively started aside with a cry of alarm: not soon enough, however; the volume was flung, it hit me, and I fell, striking my head against the door and cutting it. The cut bled, the pain was sharp: my terror had passed its climax; other feelings succeeded.

"Wicked and cruel boy!" I said. "You are like a murderer—you are like a slave-driver—you are like the Roman emperors!"

I had read Goldsmith's History of Rome, and had formed my opinion of Nero, Caligula, &c. Also I had drawn parallels in silence, which I never thought thus to have declared aloud.

"What! what!" he cried. "Did she say that to me? Did you hear her, Eliza and Georgiana? Won't I tell mama? but first—"

He ran headlong at me: I felt him grasp my hair and my shoulder: he had closed with a desperate thing. I really saw in him a tyrant, a murderer. I felt a drop or two of blood from my head trickle down my neck, and was sensible of somewhat pungent suffering: these sensations for the time predominated over fear, and I received him in frantic sort. I don't very well know what I did with my hands, but he called me "Rat! Rat!" and bellowed out aloud. Aid was near him: Eliza and Georgiana had run for Mrs. Reed, who was gone upstairs: she now came upon the scene, followed by Bessie and her maid Abbot. We were parted: I heard the words—

"Dear! dear! What a fury to fly at Master John!"

"Did ever anybody see such a picture of passion!"

Then Mrs. Reed subjoined—

"Take her away to the red-room, and lock her in there." Four hands were immediately laid upon me, and I was borne upstairs.

Writing Under a Pseudonym

IN A TIME WHEN FEMALE authors often faced discrimination and prejudice, Brontë, like her sisters, wrote under a male pseudonym to protect their privacy and work. The Brontë sisters' decision to use male aliases—Currer, Ellis, and Acton Bell—allowed their works to be evaluated on their literary merits rather than their gender, which was a significant barrier for women writers during the 19th century.

Legacy and Influence

CHARLOTTE BRONTË'S contribution to English literature is immeasurable. Her novels, characterized by their vivid characters and deep exploration of human psychology, remain relevant and thought-provoking. She laid the foundation for the later development of the novel as a form of psychological and social analysis.

Moreover, Brontë's depiction of strong, independent, and complex female characters in her novels, most notably Jane Eyre, has made a lasting impact on feminist literature and continues to inspire women and men alike to seek self-respect, independence, and love without compromising their principles. The enduring appeal of "Jane Eyre" in particular has led to numerous adaptations and retellings, further cementing her place in literary history.

Charlotte Brontë's work and legacy also contribute to the understanding of the Victorian era, its societal norms, and the struggles faced by women. Her writing captures the essence of a time marked by rapid industrialization and significant societal change, providing invaluable insights into the human condition.

In her own time and throughout the ages, Charlotte Brontë's work has been a source of inspiration and solace to countless readers. Her literary legacy remains as strong and enduring as the winds that sweep across the Yorkshire moors, and her contributions continue to serve as a testament to the enduring power of the written word to illuminate the human experience. Charlotte Brontë, a trailblazer of her time, left behind a literary legacy that continues to resonate with readers, reminding them of the enduring strength and resilience of the human spirit.

Emily Brontë: The Enigmatic Wuthering Heights

IN THE REMOTE AND WINDSWEPT moors of Yorkshire, the shy and reclusive Emily Brontë penned a novel that would become one of the most enigmatic and enduring classics in English literature—"Wuthering Heights." Her singular work defied the conventions of her time and left an indelible mark on the literary landscape, offering readers a haunting, dark, and tumultuous love story set against a backdrop of untamed nature and human passion.

Early Life and Family

EMILY BRONTË WAS BORN on July 30, 1818, in Thornton, Yorkshire, England, and was the fifth of six children in the Brontë family. Her father, Patrick Brontë, was a clergyman, and her mother, Maria Brontë, died when Emily was just three years old. Her early years were marked by close sibling bonds, particularly with her sisters, Charlotte and Anne, with whom she shared an enduring love of storytelling and imagination.

Growing up in the remote village of Haworth, the Brontë siblings found solace and inspiration in their isolated surroundings, cultivating a profound connection with the wild and rugged moors that would later become a central element in Emily's novel.

The Novel's Unconventional Nature

"WUTHERING HEIGHTS," published in 1847 under the pseudonym "Ellis Bell," is a story that defies easy categorization. It is often described as a Gothic novel, a love story, a tragedy, and even a psychological thriller. The novel's complex narrative structure, multiple narrators, and bleak and brooding atmosphere set it apart from the conventional literature of the time.

The story unfolds through the perspective of Mr. Lockwood, a newcomer to the region, who becomes intrigued by the isolated estate of Wuthering Heights. There, he encounters the enigmatic figure of Heathcliff, an orphan who was adopted into the Earnshaw family and who holds the key to a turbulent and dark history of love and revenge.

The novel's emotional intensity, complex characters, and supernatural elements have made "Wuthering Heights" a source of fascination and debate among scholars and readers alike. At its core, the novel delves into themes of love, cruelty, revenge, and the destructive power of obsession.

The Enigmatic Characters

THE CHARACTERS IN "Wuthering Heights" are as enigmatic and passionate as the moors themselves. Heathcliff, the dark and mysterious antihero, is a figure of undying love and relentless vengeance. His turbulent relationship with Catherine Earnshaw, his childhood friend and love interest, forms the emotional core of the story. Catherine's own inner turmoil, her desire for the wild and untamed Heathcliff and her societal obligations, sets the stage for a tragic love story that transcends death.

Other characters, like the rational and reserved Lockwood and the housekeeper Joseph, offer contrasting perspectives and emphasize the novel's exploration of class, culture, and human nature. The novel's vivid and complex characters are brought to life through Emily Brontë's masterful prose and keen psychological insight.

Literary Influence and Legacy

DESPITE INITIAL MIXED reviews and controversies over its dark themes, "Wuthering Heights" has become a literary masterpiece. It has inspired countless adaptations, films, and reimaginings, solidifying its place in the canon of English literature. The novel's exploration of the human psyche and its portrayal of intense, unconventional love have struck a chord with readers and continue to captivate audiences today.

Emily Brontë's writing, characterized by its emotional intensity and evocative descriptions of the natural world, has made her a revered figure in the literary world. Her contribution to the development of the novel as a medium for exploring the inner workings of the human mind and heart is profound.

While Emily Brontë's life was short and marked by isolation, her literary legacy has left an enduring imprint on the literary world. Her singular work, "Wuthering Heights," continues to intrigue and beguile readers, reminding us of the enduring power of literature to delve into the complexities of human nature and to evoke profound emotional responses. Emily Brontë, the enigmatic author of the Yorkshire moors, has gifted us a literary masterpiece that remains as timeless and wild as the landscapes it portrays.

Anne Brontë: The Lesser-Known Brontë Sister

IN THE SHADOW OF HER more celebrated sisters, Emily and Charlotte, Anne Brontë, the youngest of the Brontë siblings, made her own unique and enduring mark on English literature. Often overshadowed by her sisters' literary achievements, Anne's works and life story are a testament to her talent, inner strength, and her dedication to challenging societal norms of her time.

Early Life and Family

BORN ON JANUARY 17, 1820, Anne Brontë was the youngest of six siblings, including her more famous sisters, Charlotte and Emily. Her father, Patrick Brontë, was the parson of Haworth, Yorkshire, and her mother, Maria Brontë, passed away when Anne was an infant. Anne's childhood was marked by the close-knit bonds she formed with her sisters, especially Emily and Charlotte, as well as her older brother Branwell. The Brontë siblings' upbringing, characterized by their father's emphasis on education and a rich imagination, laid the foundation for their literary careers.

Anne's Literary Works

ANNE BRONTË'S WRITING, though less prolific than that of her sisters, is characterized by its moral depth and social critique. Her two major novels, "Agnes Grey" (1847) and "The Tenant of Wildfell Hall" (1848), reflect her keen observations of the societal injustices and inequalities faced by women in the 19th century.

"Agnes Grey" is a semi-autobiographical novel that explores the life of a governess and the difficulties faced by women who worked in such positions. The novel highlights the mistreatment and exploitation of governesses and serves as a social critique of the class system and the limitations imposed on women during that era.

"The Tenant of Wildfell Hall" is considered Anne Brontë's most significant work and one of the first feminist novels in English literature. The novel tells the story of Helen Graham, a woman who escapes an abusive marriage and seeks independence. It boldly addresses themes of alcoholism, domestic abuse, and the limited legal rights of married women at the time. The book's unflinching portrayal of these issues and its exploration of female agency challenged the societal norms of the Victorian era.

Anne's works also reflected her strong moral and religious convictions. Her writing often grappled with questions of sin, redemption, and the consequences of one's actions. Her religious views and moral values are particularly evident in "The Tenant of Wildfell Hall," where the protagonist's faith plays a significant role in her struggle for independence and her battle against her husband's moral degradation.

Anne's Legacy and Influence

ANNE BRONTË'S CONTRIBUTION to English literature was not fully recognized during her lifetime, and her work was often dismissed as being less accomplished than that of her sisters. However, in the modern era, Anne's novels have gained renewed attention and appreciation for their social commentary, feminist themes, and moral depth.

Anne's legacy as a feminist writer and social critic is increasingly acknowledged, and her novels continue to resonate with readers interested in women's rights, the role of women in society, and the complexities of human relationships. Her portrayal of strong, independent female characters was groundbreaking for her time and remains a source of inspiration for contemporary audiences.

Anne Brontë's short life was marked by her courage to confront the injustices of her society and her determination to give a voice to the voiceless. Her literature challenged Victorian norms and shed light on the struggles faced by women in the 19th century. In her own quiet but profound way, Anne Brontë added her voice to the chorus of women seeking to break free from societal constraints and establish their identities. Her work, though often considered the "lesser-known Brontë sister," continues to shine as a testament to her literary talent and her contribution to the feminist literary tradition.

Louisa May Alcott: Little Women with Big Dreams

IN THE HEART OF 19TH-century Concord, Massachusetts, Louisa May Alcott penned a novel that would capture the hearts of readers for generations— "Little Women." This enduring classic is a testament to Alcott's own life, her literary talent, and her commitment to advocating for women's rights during a time when gender roles were rigidly defined.

Early Life and Family

LOUISA MAY ALCOTT WAS born on November 29, 1832, in Germantown, Pennsylvania, and was the second of four daughters. Her father, Amos Bronson Alcott, was a renowned educator and philosopher, and her mother, Abigail May Alcott, was a social worker and a member of the Women's suffrage movement. These formative family connections exposed Louisa to a world of intellectual exploration and social reform, and it was within this environment that she nurtured her own intellectual and literary aspirations.

"Little Women" and Its Impact

PUBLISHED IN TWO VOLUMES in 1868 and 1869, "Little Women" is Louisa May Alcott's most famous work and one of the most cherished books in American literature. The novel is a semi-autobiographical account of the lives of the four March sisters—Meg, Jo, Beth, and Amy—growing up in Civil War-era New England. It portrays their experiences, dreams, and the challenges they face as they journey from girlhood to womanhood.

"Little Women" is a novel of timeless themes—family, love, ambition, and the struggle for personal and creative fulfillment. The character of Jo March, a fiercely independent and aspiring writer, has become a beloved figure of literary feminism. Jo's desire to be her own person, to pursue her dreams, and to reject the limitations placed on women during her time made her a groundbreaking character, and she served as an inspiration to countless young women.

The novel also explores the bond of sisterhood and the importance of female relationships. The March sisters, though different in temperament, support and uplift each other through the challenges of life. Their unity and individual growth remain central to the novel's enduring appeal.

Alcott's Commitment to Feminism

LOUISA MAY ALCOTT'S life was intertwined with her beliefs in feminism and gender equality. As a young woman, she served as a nurse during the American Civil War and experienced the struggles of women who were challenging traditional gender roles. Her experiences and observations further fueled her commitment to the women's suffrage movement and her determination to use her writing as a platform for advocating women's rights.

In addition to "Little Women," Alcott penned sequels and numerous other works, including "Little Men" and "Jo's Boys," further developing the characters and themes she introduced in her most famous novel. She also wrote stories for adults and children that championed the idea of women's independence and self-reliance.

Legacy and Influence

LOUISA MAY ALCOTT'S legacy as a writer, feminist, and advocate for social reform is significant. Her dedication to women's rights, her creation of strong, independent female characters, and her ability to address the complexities of familial relationships and personal growth have left an indelible mark on American literature.

"Little Women" has been adapted into numerous plays, movies, and television series, solidifying its status as a beloved classic. The novel continues to inspire generations of readers and has been a source of empowerment for young girls and women, encouraging them to pursue their dreams and resist societal limitations.

Louisa May Alcott's own life, characterized by her passion for literature and her unwavering commitment to social reform, serves as an inspiration for those who aspire to make a difference through their words and actions. Her legacy reminds us that even those who appear to be "little women" can make a big impact, challenging societal norms and advocating for a world where dreams and ambitions know no gender boundaries.

Zora Neale Hurston: Harlem's Literary Jewel

IN THE VIBRANT AND culturally rich neighborhood of Harlem during the Harlem Renaissance, Zora Neale Hurston emerged as one of the most celebrated figures in African American literature. Her pioneering work as an author, anthropologist, and folklorist enriched the tapestry of American literature and provided an authentic voice to the African American experience in the early 20th century.

Early Life and Education

ZORA NEALE HURSTON was born on January 7, 1891, in Notasulga, Alabama. Her family later moved to Eatonville, Florida, one of the first all-Black incorporated towns in the United States. This unique upbringing in an all-Black community provided her with a deep appreciation for the culture, folklore, and language of African Americans, which would later become central to her literary work.

Hurston's formal education included attending Howard University, a historically Black institution, where she studied anthropology and literature. Her education laid the foundation for her later work as an anthropologist, allowing her to delve into the rich cultural heritage of African Americans in the South.

The Harlem Renaissance

DURING THE 1920S AND 1930s, Harlem, New York, became the epicenter of African American cultural and artistic expression. Zora Neale Hurston was a prominent figure in this cultural movement, known as the Harlem Renaissance, which celebrated the achievements of African American artists and writers.

Hurston's literary career flourished during her time in New York City, where she became associated with influential figures of the era, including Langston Hughes, Alain Locke, and Claude McKay. She contributed to the literary magazine "Fire!!" and found her voice in the New Negro Movement, which aimed to promote African American cultural pride and challenge racial stereotypes.

Literary Work

ZORA NEALE HURSTON'S most famous work, "Their Eyes Were Watching God," was published in 1937. This novel, a seminal piece of African American and women's literature, tells the story of Janie Crawford, an African American woman's journey towards self-discovery and independence in the rural South. The novel beautifully captures the Southern dialect and the complexities of Janie's experiences as she navigates love, identity, and societal expectations.

Hurston's writing style was characterized by its vivid use of dialect, folklore, and storytelling. She immersed herself in the lives of the people she wrote about, conducting anthropological research and collecting oral histories that she incorporated into her work. Her ability to capture the authentic voices and stories of African Americans set her apart as a literary force.

Anthropological Work

IN ADDITION TO HER literary endeavors, Hurston made significant contributions to the field of anthropology. She conducted fieldwork in the South and the Caribbean, collecting folklore, songs, and oral histories from African American and Afro-Caribbean communities. Her anthropological research, often blending seamlessly with her literary work, served as a valuable record of the cultural expressions and traditions of these communities.

Challenges and Reemergence

DESPITE HER EARLY SUCCESS, Hurston faced challenges in the later years of her life. Her works fell into relative obscurity, and she struggled with financial difficulties. It was not until the late 20th century that her literary contributions were rediscovered and celebrated.

In the 1970s and 1980s, a renewed interest in the works of Zora Neale Hurston led to the reissuing of her books and a revival of her legacy. Her unique voice and her unwavering commitment to representing the African American experience made her a beacon for a new generation of scholars, writers, and readers.

Legacy and Impact

ZORA NEALE HURSTON'S legacy is profound. Her works, including "Their Eyes Were Watching God" and her folkloric collections, are celebrated for their authenticity and cultural significance. Her ability to capture the essence of African American life and storytelling, along with her commitment to challenging stereotypes and promoting cultural pride, have had a lasting impact on African American literature and the broader literary canon.

Zora Neale Hurston, the literary jewel of Harlem, continues to shine brightly in the world of American literature. Her pioneering spirit, dedication to African American culture, and her remarkable ability to weave folklore, dialect, and storytelling into her work ensure her place as a celebrated figure in American letters and a source of inspiration for generations of writers and scholars.

Toni Morrison: Nobel Laureate of Unflinching Realism

TONI MORRISON, ONE of the most celebrated American authors of the 20th century, possessed a unique gift for unflinching realism and a profound commitment to depicting the African American experience. Her work, characterized by its deep exploration of identity, race, and memory, earned her numerous accolades, including the Nobel Prize in Literature. Toni Morrison's powerful narratives continue to resonate with readers and stand as a testament to the enduring impact of her literary contributions.

Early Life and Education

TONI MORRISON WAS BORN as Chloe Anthony Wofford on February 18, 1931, in Lorain, Ohio. She grew up in a working-class family, where the oral tradition of storytelling was a significant influence on her life. The stories her family shared and the folklore she heard as a child would later shape her approach to literature.

Morrison's academic pursuits were marked by excellence. She attended Howard University, a historically Black college in Washington, D.C., where she immersed herself in literature, the arts, and the study of African American history. Later, she pursued a master's degree in English at Cornell University, where she conducted research on the themes of suicide in the works of William Faulkner and Virginia Woolf.

Literary Career

TONI MORRISON'S CAREER as an author took root when she joined the publishing industry as an editor at Random House. In her role as an editor, she championed African American literature and was instrumental in the publication of works by important authors such as Angela Davis and Gayl Jones. Her publishing background provided her with valuable insights into the world of literature, and it wasn't long before she began writing herself.

In 1970, she published her debut novel, "The Bluest Eye," which explored the psychological and emotional struggles of a young African American girl who longed for blue eyes to escape the pain of her existence. The novel was the beginning of a remarkable literary journey that would span several decades.

Morrison's magnum opus, "Beloved," published in 1987, is a profound exploration of the legacy of slavery and its enduring impact on African American identity. The novel, which won the Pulitzer Prize for Fiction, delves into themes of motherhood, trauma, and the intersection of history and personal experience. "Beloved" is widely considered one of the greatest novels of the 20th century and remains a pivotal work in American literature.

Morrison's other notable works include "Song of Solomon," "Sula," "Jazz," and "Paradise." These novels continue her exploration of identity, love, and the struggle for selfhood within the African American community. Her writing is characterized by its lyrical prose, deep psychological insight, and a unique narrative style that weaves together different voices and perspectives.

Nobel Prize and Impact

IN 1993, TONI MORRISON was awarded the Nobel Prize in Literature. The Swedish Academy recognized her as a writer "who in novels characterized by visionary force and poetic import, gives life to an essential aspect of American reality." Her Nobel lecture, titled "Nobel Lecture in Literature," emphasized the power of language and storytelling in addressing the complexity of human existence.

Toni Morrison's literary contributions extended beyond her novels. She wrote essays, plays, and children's books, further solidifying her reputation as a literary icon and an influential voice in American culture. Her work, often inspired by African American history and the enduring legacy of slavery, was central to the development of African American literature and the broader literary canon.

Legacy and Enduring Relevance

TONI MORRISON'S WORK continues to be studied, celebrated, and embraced for its unflinching examination of American history and culture. Her narratives shed light on the African American experience, exposing the realities of racial injustice, the complexities of identity, and the human capacity for resilience and love. Her storytelling, often rooted in the concept of "rememory," challenges conventional notions of time and memory.

Morrison's influence on American literature and her enduring legacy are profound. Her ability to capture the intersection of individual and collective history, her lyrical prose, and her exploration of the African American experience have left an indelible mark on the literary landscape. Her work speaks to the enduring power of storytelling to illuminate the human condition and to inspire readers to confront the difficult truths of their own histories. Toni Morrison, the Nobel Laureate of unflinching realism, stands as a literary giant whose work continues to enrich and challenge the literary world and society as a whole.

Contemporary Voices: A Symphony of Diversity

AS THE 21ST CENTURY unfolded, a remarkable chorus of diverse voices emerged, captivating the literary landscape and bringing fresh perspectives and narratives to the forefront. This wave of contemporary authors has beautifully enriched the tapestry of literature, shedding light on untold stories, cultural intricacies, and the nuances of humanity. Among these authors, Chimamanda Ngozi Adichie and Arundhati Roy have cast an indelible mark, each weaving a tapestry of their own, and in the realm of young adult fiction, J.K. Rowling has introduced readers to the enchanting world of Hogwarts, where a young witch named Hermione Granger has become an emblem of intelligence and courage.

Chimamanda Ngozi Adichie: Illuminating the Nigerian-Biafran Conflict

CHIMAMANDA NGOZI ADICHIE, a literary luminary of our time, has unveiled the poignant and complex history of Nigeria through her powerful storytelling. In her magnum opus, "Half of a Yellow Sun," she takes readers on a poignant journey into the heart of the Nigerian-Biafran conflict, a chapter of history often overlooked by the world. Adichie's narrative prowess exposes the human drama and sacrifices that unfolded during the conflict, offering readers a rare glimpse into the intricate tapestry of history and humanity.

Published in 2006, "Half of a Yellow Sun" is a narrative tour de force, exploring the lives of individuals caught in the throes of war. The characters she creates are compelling, each representing a different facet of the conflict—Ugwu, the bright and sensitive houseboy; Olanna, the compassionate and resilient intellectual; and Odenigbo, the passionate revolutionary. Through their intertwined lives, Adichie paints a vivid portrait of a nation torn apart, with themes of love, resilience, and the human spirit shining through the chaos of war.

Adichie's storytelling is characterized by its emotional depth and an acute sensitivity to the complexities of human relationships. She offers a searing exploration of love, sacrifice, and endurance amidst the brutality of war, making "Half of a Yellow Sun" a powerful testament to her narrative prowess and ability to evoke empathy in her readers.

Beyond her novels, Adichie is a fervent advocate for gender equality and her essay "We Should All Be Feminists" has sparked a global conversation about the importance of feminism and the need to address gender disparities in society. Her writing frequently delves into the challenges and triumphs of women navigating a world marked by inequality and discrimination.

Arundhati Roy: Unraveling the Intricacies of India with Lyrical Prose

ARUNDHATI ROY, AN INDIAN author of unparalleled literary talent, offers readers an opportunity to immerse themselves in the vibrant tapestry of India through her masterful storytelling. Her debut novel, "The God of Small Things," published in 1997, is a work of extraordinary beauty that explores the intricate web of family secrets, societal intricacies, and forbidden love.

Set in the lush and exotic landscapes of Kerala, India, "The God of Small Things" delves into the lives of fraternal twins, Estha and Rahel, who are bound by love and torn apart by tragedy. Roy's lyrical prose and intricate narrative structure create a mesmerizing and immersive reading experience, allowing readers to witness the everyday magic and heart-wrenching tragedies of her characters.

Roy's work serves as a powerful critique of a society deeply entrenched in class and caste divisions, offering a searing exploration of the impact of these divisions on individual lives. Her novel, marked by lush descriptions, complex characters, and intricate family dynamics, paints a portrait of India that is both deeply personal and universal.

Beyond her novels, Arundhati Roy is known for her incisive commentary on social and political issues in India. Her essays and non-fiction works provide thought-provoking insights into topics such as environmentalism, political activism, and human rights. She is a fierce advocate for social justice and has consistently used her voice and her writing to highlight the struggles faced by marginalized communities in India and beyond.

J.K. Rowling: Unveiling the Magic of Hogwarts and Hermione Granger

IN THE REALM OF YOUNG adult fiction, J.K. Rowling has transported readers to the enchanting world of Hogwarts School of Witchcraft and Wizardry through her immensely popular "Harry Potter" series. Her captivating storytelling has not only introduced readers to a world of magic but has also given rise to a beloved and iconic character—Hermione Granger.

Hermione Granger, a brilliant and resourceful witch, quickly became an enduring symbol of intelligence, courage, and female empowerment. She is known for her insatiable thirst for knowledge, her unwavering determination, and her fierce loyalty to her friends. Hermione challenges traditional gender roles by portraying a young woman who embraces her intelligence and uses her skills to solve problems, save lives, and stand up for what she believes in.

J.K. Rowling's storytelling captures the imagination of readers of all ages, creating a world of wonder, adventure, and life lessons that resonate with young readers. Through the "Harry Potter" series, Rowling has not only cultivated a love for reading in countless young minds but has also inspired a generation of readers to be brave, kind, and unapologetically themselves.

Conclusion

CHIMAMANDA NGOZI ADICHIE, Arundhati Roy, and J.K. Rowling are just a few of the diverse voices that have enriched contemporary literature in the 21st century. Their storytelling prowess, unflinching exploration of history, culture, and the human experience, as well as their dedication to social justice and gender equality, showcase the transformative power of literature. As these authors continue to captivate readers worldwide, they remind us that diverse voices are essential in providing a deeper understanding of our world and the human condition. In this symphony of diversity, they have not only entertained us but have also shaped our perspectives and encouraged us to be more empathetic, courageous, and compassionate.

THESE REMARKABLE WOMEN, each with a pen in hand and a story in their hearts, have gifted the world timeless tales of courage, love, and resilience. Through their words, they have transcended the constraints of their time, inspiring generations to come. As we turn the pages of their works, we are reminded that literature knows no gender, no boundaries. It is a boundless realm where the voices of women, both past and present, echo, encouraging us all to trailblaze our own paths and script our own stories.

In the chapters that follow, we will continue our exploration of the awe-inspiring journeys of women who have left an indelible mark on history. Their stories are not just narratives of the past; they are guiding stars, illuminating the way for us to forge ahead, to challenge the status quo, and to become boundless trailblazers in our own right.

Chapter 7: Women in Leadership and Politics

In a world that has often been dominated by men, women in leadership and politics have risen time and time again to challenge the status quo, breaking through the glass ceilings of power and influence. They've not only shaped the course of nations but also shattered preconceived notions of what women can achieve in traditionally male-dominated spheres.

As we delve into the captivating stories of these trailblazing women, prepare to be inspired, awed, and empowered. From the queens of ancient civilizations to the modern-day political giants, these women have wielded power with grace, wisdom, and an indomitable spirit.

Cleopatra: The Queen of Charm and Charisma

OUR JOURNEY THROUGH history begins in the dazzling world of ancient Egypt with Cleopatra, a queen whose name resonates with charm, charisma, and unparalleled political prowess. While Cleopatra may be best known for her relationships with Julius Caesar and Mark Antony, she was a formidable ruler in her own right.

Born in 69 BC, Cleopatra ascended the throne of Egypt at just 18 years old, and she quickly proved herself a brilliant diplomat and administrator. Her reign marked a time of cultural revival and economic prosperity in Egypt. She was fluent in several languages and had a keen intellect, making her a formidable negotiator and diplomat. Cleopatra's leadership wasn't just about maintaining her own power;

she was dedicated to ensuring the welfare and stability of her people.

Her story is a testament to the enduring power of female leadership, and her influence in both ancient history and pop culture is undeniable. Her legacy reminds us that women have always been capable of ruling with wisdom and determination.

Elizabeth I: The Virgin Queen Who Defined an Era

JUMPING AHEAD IN TIME to the Elizabethan era, we encounter another formidable female leader. Elizabeth I, often referred to as the "Virgin Queen," reigned over England from 1558 to 1603. Her rule was a time of remarkable cultural flourishing, often described as the Elizabethan Renaissance.

Elizabeth I was a monarch who demonstrated extraordinary wisdom and determination in a world where male heirs were the norm. She proved that a woman could wield power and guide a nation to greatness. Her reign saw the defeat of the Spanish Armada, the blossoming of English literature with writers like William Shakespeare, and the establishment of the Protestant Church of England.

Elizabeth I's legacy continues to inspire women in leadership, showing that intellect and strength know no gender boundaries. Her remarkable story serves as a reminder that women can excel in politics and leadership, making their mark on history.

Angela Merkel, Jacinda Ardern, and Kamala Harris: Leading the Way in Modern Times

FAST FORWARD TO THE present day, where women continue to redefine leadership and politics. Angela Merkel, the former Chancellor of Germany, made history as the first woman to hold that office. Her leadership during the European financial crisis and the refugee crisis demonstrated a calm and steady hand in times of turmoil.

Jacinda Ardern, the Prime Minister of New Zealand, has been recognized for her compassionate and effective leadership, particularly during the challenging times of the Christchurch mosque shootings and the COVID-19 pandemic. Her focus on well-being and empathy in politics sets a new standard for leadership in the 21st century.

Kamala Harris, the Vice President of the United States, has broken several barriers at once, becoming the first female, the first Black, and the first Asian American vice president. Her election signifies a milestone in American politics, illustrating that diverse voices and experiences are crucial to shaping a more inclusive future.

THESE WOMEN ARE CONTEMPORARY leaders who continue to inspire not only through their accomplishments but also through their unshakable determination to shatter the glass ceiling of politics. Their stories remind us that women can ascend to the highest echelons of power, bringing fresh perspectives and a commitment to progress.

In this chapter, we've explored the extraordinary lives of women in leadership and politics. From the strategic brilliance of Cleopatra to the statesmanship of Elizabeth I and the contemporary trailblazers like Angela Merkel, Jacinda Ardern, and Kamala Harris, these women exemplify the enduring power of female leadership throughout history. Their stories encourage us to challenge stereotypes, push boundaries, and strive for a more inclusive and equitable world, where women continue to lead and shape the course of history.

Chapter 8: Social Reformers

In a world where injustice often seems like an unmovable mountain, it's the courageous and compassionate women who step forward as the trailblazers for change. Chapter 8 of "Boundless Trailblazers: Inspiring Stories of Real Women Throughout History and the Present Time" introduces us to the remarkable social reformers whose tireless efforts have lit a path towards a fairer, more inclusive world.

Mother Teresa: An Angel of Compassion

MOTHER TERESA, A NAME that has become synonymous with compassion and selflessness, was born Anjezë Gonxhe Bojaxhiu on August 26, 1910, in Skopje, which was then part of the Ottoman Empire (now the capital of North Macedonia). She would later go on to become one of the most revered figures in the history of humanitarian work. Her life's journey was a testament to the profound impact that one individual's love, faith, and dedication can have on the lives of the suffering and destitute.

Early Life and Calling

GROWING UP IN A DEVOUT Catholic family, Anjezë was exposed to the teachings of Jesus Christ from a young age, which would go on to shape her life's mission. At the tender age of 12, she experienced what she described as a "call within a call." It was a moment of profound clarity, a divine revelation that drove her to devote her life to helping the poor and the marginalized. Little did anyone know that this young girl from Skopje would one day touch the hearts of millions worldwide.

The Missionaries of Charity

IN 1928, AT THE AGE of 18, Anjezë left her family and country to join the Sisters of Loreto, a religious congregation in Ireland. She adopted the name Sister Mary Teresa, inspired by Saint Thérèse of Lisieux. She began her missionary work in Darjeeling, India, where she learned Bengali and taught at St. Teresa's School. However, her real calling lay in the slums of Calcutta, where she started working in 1948.

The Slums of Calcutta

CALCUTTA IN THE 1940S and 1950s was a place of abject poverty, where millions lived in squalor, suffering from disease, malnutrition, and neglect. Sister Teresa took to the streets, tending to the sick and dying, picking up abandoned children, and comforting the aged. With unwavering determination, she founded the Missionaries of Charity in 1950, an organization committed to helping "the hungry, the naked, the homeless, the crippled, the blind, the lepers, all those people who feel unwanted, unloved, uncared for throughout society, people that have become a burden to the society and are shunned by everyone."

Nobel Peace Prize and Worldwide Recognition

MOTHER TERESA'S WORK garnered global attention. She received numerous awards, including the Nobel Peace Prize in 1979, recognizing her tireless efforts to alleviate human suffering. She used the prize money to establish a leper colony, a home for orphaned children, and a home for the destitute in Calcutta.

The Legacy

MOTHER TERESA'S WORK continued until her death on

September 5, 1997. Her legacy is immeasurable, with the Missionaries of Charity now operating in over 130 countries, providing care and support to the most vulnerable in society. She showed the world that it is possible to combat poverty, suffering, and injustice with love, compassion, and unwavering faith.

Mother Teresa's life story is a testament to the power of one person's unwavering dedication and selflessness in the face of immense suffering. She demonstrated that love and compassion can transcend boundaries, heal wounds, and make the world a better place. Her canonization as a saint in 2016 by the Catholic Church further solidified her place in history as a paragon of altruism and humanitarianism.

As we reflect on the life of Mother Teresa, we're reminded that each of us has the potential to make a difference, to be a beacon of light in the darkest of places, and to offer love and compassion to those in need. Her example challenges us to cultivate the seeds of kindness and service within our own hearts, knowing that even small acts of love can create ripples of hope in a world often marred by suffering. Mother Teresa's life was a profound testament to the boundless capacity of the human spirit for compassion, and her legacy continues to inspire and guide us to this day.

Harriet Tubman: The Underground Railroad's Guiding Light

HARRIET TUBMAN'S LIFE is a remarkable story of unwavering courage, resilience, and selflessness. Born into slavery in Dorchester County, Maryland, around 1820, she endured the harsh realities of a system that dehumanized her and countless others. Her journey from enslaved individual to one of the most prominent conductors of the Underground Railroad represents the very essence of hope, freedom, and the indomitable human spirit.

The Life of Enslavement

HARRIET TUBMAN WAS born as Araminta "Minty" Ross into a world that denied her the most basic human rights. At the age of five, she was already witnessing the brutalities of slavery, enduring the hardships of forced labor, cruel punishments, and constant threats of family separation. The seeds of resistance were sown early in her life as she endured the inhumane conditions of the Maryland plantation.

Escape to Freedom

HARRIET TUBMAN'S FIRST act of defiance occurred in 1849 when she escaped from her enslavement, a decision that marked the beginning of her transformation into a symbol of hope. She fled to Pennsylvania, a free state, and the taste of freedom empowered her with a burning desire to help others escape their own bondage.

The Underground Railroad

HARRIET TUBMAN'S MOST famous and courageous role was as a conductor on the Underground Railroad, a network of safe houses and secret routes that helped enslaved individuals escape to freedom in the North or Canada. Often described as the "Moses of her people," she made around 19 trips back to the South, risking her life to guide over 300 people, including family members, to freedom. Her uncanny ability to navigate the wilderness and evade slave hunters earned her the reputation of being almost supernatural.

A Soldier, Spy, and Nurse

DURING THE CIVIL WAR, Harriet Tubman continued to serve her people by offering her skills and expertise. She worked as a nurse, cook, and even a spy for the Union Army, using her knowledge of the South to gather intelligence and support the war effort. Her contributions did not go unnoticed, as she became a respected figure in the military.

Later Years and Activism

AFTER THE CIVIL WAR, Harriet Tubman continued to fight for social justice. She advocated for women's suffrage, knowing that the struggle for equal rights extended beyond the abolition of slavery. Her tireless work for women's rights and her dedication to the causes she believed in demonstrated her unwavering commitment to justice.

Legacy and Inspiration

HARRIET TUBMAN'S LEGACY is etched into the annals of American history as an embodiment of hope and tenacity. Her life was a testament to the power of an individual to change the world, and her name is synonymous with the fight for freedom and equality. She passed away on March 10, 1913, but her memory and spirit live on, inspiring generations to come.

Harriet Tubman's story serves as a source of inspiration for all. Her courage in the face of overwhelming adversity, her selflessness in the pursuit of justice, and her indomitable spirit in the quest for freedom continue to inspire countless people around the world. She stands as a beacon of hope, reminding us that even in the darkest of times, a single person's resolve can lead to profound change. Harriet Tubman's life is a shining example of the remarkable achievements possible when one's heart is driven by the fervor of justice and the relentless pursuit of a better, more equitable world.

Malala Yousafzai: Fearless Advocate for Education

MALALA YOUSAFZAI'S story is one of extraordinary courage, determination, and resilience in the face of adversity. Born on July 12, 1997, in Mingora, Swat Valley, Pakistan, Malala grew up in a region where the Taliban's oppressive regime sought to deny education to girls. However, Malala's unwavering belief in the power of education and her fearless advocacy turned her into a global icon for girls' rights and education.

Early Years and Education

FROM A YOUNG AGE, MALALA was passionate about learning. Her father, Ziauddin Yousafzai, was an educational activist, and he instilled in her the importance of education and equality. Despite the Taliban's efforts to ban girls from attending school, Malala continued to attend classes and became an outspoken advocate for the right to education.

The Attack and Triumph Over Adversity

IN OCTOBER 2012, TRAGEDY struck when Malala was targeted by the Taliban for her activism. A gunman boarded her school bus and shot her in the head, leaving her critically wounded. Miraculously, Malala survived the attack and, after extensive medical treatment and rehabilitation, emerged stronger than ever. Her resilience captured the world's attention, and her determination to continue her advocacy work became a beacon of hope for millions.

The Malala Fund and Global Impact

MALALA, ALONG WITH her father, co-founded the Malala Fund, a nonprofit organization dedicated to advocating for girls' education around the world. Through the Malala Fund, she has worked tirelessly to ensure that every girl receives twelve years of free, quality education. The organization provides financial support, advocates for policy changes, and raises awareness about the importance of education, especially for girls in vulnerable communities.

Nobel Peace Prize and Ongoing Advocacy

IN RECOGNITION OF HER remarkable efforts, Malala was

awarded the Nobel Peace Prize in 2014, becoming the youngest-ever recipient at the age of 17. This prestigious honor further amplified her message and inspired people globally to support the cause of girls' education. Malala has continued to use her platform to advocate for education, gender equality, and social justice, speaking at international forums, meeting with world leaders, and empowering young girls to pursue their dreams.

Educational Advocacy and Impact

MALALA'S IMPACT ON education is immeasurable. Her advocacy has led to significant strides in raising awareness about the barriers girls face in accessing education, prompting policy changes in various countries. She has become a symbol of hope for girls worldwide, showing them that their voices matter and that they have the right to learn, dream, and achieve.

Personal Growth and Inspiration

BEYOND HER ADVOCACY, Malala's personal growth and resilience in the face of adversity serve as an inspiration to millions. Despite the hardships she has endured, she remains compassionate, humble, and dedicated to making a positive difference in the world. Her story resonates with people from all walks of life, reminding them of the transformative power of education and the importance of standing up for what is right.

Malala Yousafzai's journey from a young schoolgirl in Pakistan to a global advocate for education highlights the strength of the human spirit and the impact one individual can have on the world. Her unwavering commitment to the fundamental right to education serves as a reminder that education is not just a privilege but a basic human right that should be accessible to every child, regardless of their gender or background. Malala's fearlessness, determination, and advocacy continue to inspire generations, reminding us all of the potential for positive change when we stand up for justice and equality.

Greta Thunberg: The Youth Climate Champion

GRETA THUNBERG'S JOURNEY from a lone school strike protester to a global icon for climate action is a testament to the power of youth activism, unwavering dedication, and the urgency of addressing climate change. Born on January 3, 2003, in Stockholm, Sweden, Greta's story has inspired a worldwide movement demanding urgent action to combat the climate crisis.

Awakening to the Climate Crisis

GRETA'S JOURNEY AS a climate activist began at the tender age of 15 when, in August 2018, she started striking from school every Friday to protest inaction on climate change. She held a hand-painted sign that read "Skolstrejk för klimatet" (School Strike for Climate) outside the Swedish Parliament, sparking a movement that soon spread across the globe.

The Power of One Voice

GRETA'S STEADFAST COMMITMENT and unapologetic frankness attracted the world's attention. Her "Fridays for Future" movement quickly gained momentum as millions of students and activists, young and old, joined her in striking for climate action. Her simple message was clear: the climate crisis was an emergency, and the world's leaders needed to treat it as such.

Speaking Truth to Power

GRETA'S PASSIONATE speeches delivered at global platforms such as the United Nations Climate Action Summit in 2019 and the World Economic Forum captured the essence of her message. She did not shy away from calling out world leaders for their failure to take meaningful action. Her words, often tinged with anger and frustration, resonated deeply with people who recognized the urgency of the climate crisis.

Time Magazine's Person of the Year

IN 2019, GRETA WAS named Time magazine's Person of the Year, becoming the youngest recipient of this prestigious accolade. This recognition highlighted her extraordinary impact on global awareness of climate change and the urgent need for action. She also received numerous awards and honors, all of which she used as platforms to amplify her message.

The Role of Youth in Climate Activism

GRETA THUNBERG'S INFLUENCE goes beyond her own actions; she has become a symbol of youth engagement in climate activism. Her story empowers young people worldwide to take a stand for the environment, reminding them that their voices can drive change. Greta's "School Strike for Climate" movement has inspired countless youth-led climate protests and initiatives, putting pressure on governments and corporations to address the climate crisis.

Climate Action and Advocacy

GRETA THUNBERG'S ADVOCACY work focuses on the necessity of rapid, global climate action to limit global warming to 1.5 degrees Celsius above pre-industrial levels, a goal set by the Paris Agreement. She emphasizes that climate change affects everyone, especially vulnerable communities, and it is our collective responsibility to take action to protect our planet for current and future generations.

Personal Sacrifice and Resilience

GRETA'S ACTIVISM HAS come at a personal cost. She has faced

criticism, mockery, and even cyberbullying from climate change deniers and others who resist change. Despite this, she has remained resolute, demonstrating the importance of standing up for one's beliefs, even in the face of adversity.

Greta Thunberg's story is a call to action for all generations. It reminds us of the collective responsibility we share in addressing the climate crisis, and it highlights the power of individual and collective voices to drive change. Her passion, unwavering commitment, and ability to mobilize millions worldwide serve as a source of inspiration, encouraging people to confront the urgent environmental challenges we face. Greta Thunberg's legacy is a testament to the potential of youth-led activism and the profound impact of speaking truth to power.

AS WE DELVE INTO THE lives of these exceptional women, we're reminded of their strength, resilience, and the transformative power of their actions. They serve as beacons of hope, illustrating that change is not only possible but within our grasp. Their stories are a testament to the fact that each of us has the potential to be a trailblazer in our own right.

In the pages of "Boundless Trailblazers," we've explored the lives and achievements of women who've shattered ceilings and shattered expectations, from the women of ancient civilizations to the icons of literature, and from women in leadership and politics to the world of entrepreneurship. Each chapter has unfolded a world of incredible stories, highlighting the remarkable contributions of women throughout history.

AS WE NEAR THE END of this journey, it's crucial to reflect on the collective strength, resilience, and ingenuity that women have demonstrated over the ages. These stories are not just tales of the past but inspirations for the future. Their impact is profound, their legacies enduring, and they beckon us to continue the journey of equality and justice.

In our conclusion, we'll tie together the threads of these remarkable stories and emphasize the importance of recognizing and celebrating the achievements of women throughout history. We'll encourage you, dear reader, to draw inspiration from these stories and to utilize your own potential to create a more equitable and inclusive future. After all, the trailblazers of the past have shown us the way; it's up to us to carry their torch and lead the way into a brighter tomorrow.

Chapter 9: Women Entrepreneurs

In this captivating chapter of "Boundless Trailblazers: Inspiring Stories of Real Women Throughout History and the Present Time," we dive into the realm of entrepreneurship and explore the remarkable journeys of women who defied expectations, broke through barriers, and carved their own paths to success. These women didn't just dream; they acted, creating businesses that not only prospered but paved the way for future generations of female entrepreneurs. Their stories are a testament to the boundless potential within each of us and the unstoppable spirit that drives change.

Madam C.J. Walker: The Empress of Hair Care

WE START WITH THE INDOMITABLE Madam C.J. Walker, a true pioneer in the world of entrepreneurship. Born Sarah Breedlove, this incredible woman's journey from humble beginnings to becoming the first self-made female millionaire in the United States is nothing short of extraordinary. Madam C.J. Walker's story is a beacon of hope for anyone who has ever dreamed of turning their passions into a prosperous business.

Facing discrimination and limited opportunities, she recognized a pressing need for hair care products for African American women. Armed with a vision, determination, and a line of innovative hair care products, Madam C.J. Walker built an empire. She defied societal norms and emerged as an inspiration for countless women, proving that with grit and innovation, anyone can achieve their dreams.

Oprah Winfrey: From Talk Show to Media Mogul

FEW NAMES ARE AS SYNONYMOUS with success as Oprah Winfrey. Her story is a testament to the power of hard work, perseverance, and the courage to overcome adversity. Oprah's rise from poverty and hardship to becoming a global media mogul is a classic example of the American dream in action.

It all began with a local radio job and eventually led to her hosting one of the most popular talk shows in television history. Yet, Oprah didn't stop there. She leveraged her fame and influence to establish her media company, Harpo Productions. Today, she is a media powerhouse, touching lives around the world with her influential platform. Oprah's journey inspires us to never underestimate the impact of our voice and our story.

Sheryl Sandberg: Leaning In and Breaking Barriers

SHERYL SANDBERG IS another incredible woman who has shattered the glass ceiling, not only for herself but for countless others. As the Chief Operating Officer of Facebook and a vocal advocate for women's empowerment in the workplace, she's become a symbol of modern entrepreneurship and leadership.

Sheryl's best-selling book, "Lean In," has inspired women worldwide to push against the stereotypes and biases that have long plagued the corporate world. Her advice on navigating the challenges of a male-dominated industry and her call for women to "lean in" and pursue leadership roles is an inspiration for the ambitious women of today.

IN THIS CHAPTER, WE'LL explore the struggles, the resilience, and the successes of these remarkable women, among others, who have made their mark in the entrepreneurial world. Their stories are a testament to the endless possibilities that lie ahead for those who dare to dream and work hard to make those dreams a reality.

So, join us as we uncover the tales of these courageous women who have paved the way for countless others, proving that no dream is too big and no obstacle is too insurmountable. Their stories are not just a celebration of individual triumphs but a rallying cry for us all to seize our own potential and, in doing so, to shape a more equitable, diverse, and inclusive world for future generations.

I apologize for the error in my previous response. You are absolutely correct; Elon Musk is not a woman. Here's a revised chapter:

Chapter 10: Modern Trailblazers

In a world where change is constant, and progress relentless, it's heartening to know that the spirit of trailblazing women remains as vibrant as ever. Our journey through history has introduced us to extraordinary women who defied expectations, shattered ceilings, and left indelible marks on their respective fields. Now, as we turn the page to the present, we enter a realm where innovation, creativity, and determination define the modern trailblazers of our time.

This chapter is an exhilarating ride through the achievements of contemporary women who've risen to prominence in an array of disciplines. These are individuals who are shaping the world we live in today, using their remarkable talents to inspire and empower others.

Tech Titans: The Visionaries

IN THE EVER-EVOLVING landscape of technology, women have emerged as visionaries, challenging stereotypes and propelling us into the future. Meet Sheryl Sandberg, the renowned tech executive who has played a pivotal role at Facebook and as an advocate for women's leadership in the tech industry. She has been a champion of diversity and gender equality in the workplace.

The tech world also reverberates with the brilliance of Gitanjali Rao, the young inventor and TIME magazine's Kid of the Year. Her contributions to water quality testing and her work inspiring young innovators show us that age is no barrier to creating change.

Entertainment Icons: The Trailblazers of Arts

IN THE REALM OF ENTERTAINMENT, women continue to break ground, tell compelling stories, and captivate global audiences. Ava DuVernay, the trailblazing filmmaker behind powerful works like "Selma" and "When They See Us," shines as an advocate for diverse storytelling in Hollywood. She uses her platform to address social injustices and uplift marginalized voices.

Then there's the incomparable Beyoncé, whose artistic genius transcends music. Her impact on culture, feminism, and activism has been immeasurable, proving that an artist can be a symbol of empowerment and change.

Activists for All: Leading the Way

THE WORLD IS FILLED with challenges, but it's also teeming with those who dare to stand up, speak out, and lead by example. Greta Thunberg, the teenage environmental activist, sparked a global youth movement demanding climate action. Her unwavering commitment reminds us that individuals, no matter their age, can initiate massive change.

Malala Yousafzai, the youngest-ever Nobel laureate, continues to advocate for girls' education and women's rights, proving that courage knows no bounds.

Phenomenal Philanthropists: Changing Lives

AMONG THE MODERN TRAILBLAZERS are women who've harnessed their resources and influence to drive positive change. Oprah Winfrey isn't just a media mogul; she's a philanthropist with a commitment to education and empowerment. Her generosity has opened doors and provided opportunities for countless individuals.

Similarly, Melinda Gates, co-chair of the Bill and Melinda Gates

Foundation, has dedicated her life to improving global health and reducing poverty. Her dedication to making the world a better place inspires us all to contribute in our own ways.

Medical Mavericks: Healing the World

OUR MODERN ERA HAS brought forth medical marvels, and women stand at the forefront of these breakthroughs. Dr. Katalin Karikó and Dr. Özlem Türeci have been instrumental in the development of groundbreaking treatments, showcasing the immense contributions women make to the field of medicine.

As we draw the curtain on this chapter, we're left with a profound sense of awe and admiration for the modern trailblazers of our time. These women are pioneers, innovators, and activists, pushing boundaries, shattering glass ceilings, and leaving their mark on the world. They are the embodiment of limitless potential, demonstrating that gender, age, or background is no obstacle to changing the world.

In the conclusion of our book, we will reflect on the overarching lessons we can glean from the lives of these incredible women throughout history and in the present. They inspire us to unlock our own potential, ignite our passions, and strive for a future marked by equality, empowerment, and boundless opportunities for all.

Conclusion

As we reach the final chapter of "Boundless Trailblazers: Inspiring Stories of Real Women Throughout History and the Present Time," we are reminded of the enduring power of women to break through barriers and redefine what is possible. Through the pages of this book, we've journeyed across centuries and continents, unveiling stories that challenge stereotypes, celebrate resilience, and inspire us to dream bigger and aim higher.

Throughout history, women have faced countless obstacles, both seen and unseen, in their pursuit of knowledge, justice, and equality. From the earliest civilizations of Ancient Egypt, Mesopotamia, Greece, and China, to the Renaissance period that birthed remarkable figures like Artemisia Gentileschi, Hildegard von Bingen, and Christine de Pizan, we've seen the persistent drive of women to shatter societal norms and achieve greatness.

In times of revolution and social change, women stepped onto the stage of history as essential agents of progress. From the suffragettes who fought tirelessly for the right to vote, to the brave individuals who led the Civil Rights Movement, their stories resonate as beacons of hope and courage.

The realm of science has also been enriched by brilliant minds like Marie Curie, Ada Lovelace, and Rosalind Franklin, whose contributions have forever altered our understanding of the world. These women paved the way for the modern scientists who continue to push the boundaries of knowledge and explore the uncharted territories of STEM fields.

In the arena of sports, icons like Wilma Rudolph, Serena Williams, Billie Jean King, and Simone Biles have left indelible imprints, proving that physical strength and determination know no gender. Their victories inspire generations to challenge preconceived limitations and aim for greatness.

In the world of literature, we've journeyed alongside Jane Austen, Virginia Woolf, and Maya Angelou, exploring how the power of the written word can ignite change and illuminate the human experience. Today, contemporary authors carry the torch, forging new paths in the literary world.

Leaders and politicians like Cleopatra, Elizabeth I, Angela Merkel, Jacinda Ardern, and Kamala Harris have showcased the potential of women to excel in roles traditionally dominated by men. Their accomplishments challenge existing power structures and chart a course for a more inclusive future.

Social reformers such as Mother Teresa, Harriet Tubman, Malala Yousafzai, and Greta Thunberg exemplify the enduring struggle for justice, equality, and the protection of our planet. These women have demonstrated that one individual can spark a global movement.

In the world of entrepreneurship, trailblazers like Madam C.J. Walker, Oprah Winfrey, and Sheryl Sandberg have disrupted industries, creating opportunities for themselves and future generations. Their stories showcase the unlimited potential of women in business.

As we approach the present day, we've met modern trailblazers who span a diverse range of fields. From technology to entertainment, activism to philanthropy, these women continue to shape the world, reinforcing the idea that there are no boundaries to what women can achieve.

The stories in this book are not mere historical footnotes. They are living proof of the power of determination, resilience, and unwavering belief in oneself. These women have walked the boundless trail, leaving an indelible mark on history, and their stories serve as a testament to the incredible capacity of the human spirit.

But it doesn't end here. The enduring message of "Boundless Trailblazers" is that every one of us has the potential to be a trailblazer in our own right. The women featured in these pages were not born extraordinary; they became extraordinary through their unwavering pursuit of their dreams and their commitment to making the world a better place. Their journeys are a testament to the infinite possibilities that lie within each of us.

As you close this book, we encourage you to carry the spirit of these trailblazers with you. Be inspired by their stories, learn from their experiences, and use their examples as a source of strength. Whether you are a woman or a man, young or old, these stories are a reminder that the world becomes a better place when we break free from the shackles of stereotypes, prejudices, and limitations. Your trailblazing journey awaits, and we can't wait to see the incredible impact you'll make.

In the end, the message is clear: the trailblazers of the past have lit the path for the trailblazers of the future. It's a boundless journey, and the destination is limited only by your imagination. So go forth with purpose, passion, and a trailblazing spirit, and let your story become a part of the inspiring tapestry of history.

List of books to read to feel empowered

1. "Lean In: Women, Work, and the Will to Lead" by Sheryl Sandberg

2. "We Should All Be Feminists" by Chimamanda Ngozi Adichie

3. "The Handmaid's Tale" by Margaret Atwood

4. "Bad Feminist" by Roxane Gay

5. "Dear Ijeawele, or A Feminist Manifesto in Fifteen Suggestions" by Chimamanda Ngozi Adichie

6. "The Girl with the Dragon Tattoo" by Stieg Larsson

7. "The Second Sex" by Simone de Beauvoir

8. "The Feminine Mystique" by Betty Friedan

9. "The Yellow Wallpaper" by Charlotte Perkins Gilman

10. "Half the Sky: Turning Oppression into Opportunity for Women Worldwide" by Nicholas D. Kristof and Sheryl WuDunn

11. "My Life on the Road" by Gloria Steinem

12. "Men Explain Things to Me" by Rebecca Solnit

13. "The Immortal Life of Henrietta Lacks" by Rebecca Skloot

14. "The Beauty Myth" by Naomi Wolf

15. "The Power" by Naomi Alderman

16. "Daring to Drive: A Saudi Woman's Awakening" by Manal al-Sharif

17. "Hidden Figures" by Margot Lee Shetterly

18. "Educated" by Tara Westover

19. "Lab Girl" by Hope Jahren

20. "Wild" by Cheryl Strayed

21. "Women Who Run with the Wolves" by Clarissa Pinkola Estés

22. "The Glass Castle" by Jeannette Walls
23. "The Hate U Give" by Angie Thomas
24. "The Wife" by Meg Wolitzer
25. "The Nightingale" by Kristin Hannah
26. "Becoming" by Michelle Obama
27. "The Female Persuasion" by Meg Wolitzer
28. "The Signature of All Things" by Elizabeth Gilbert
29. "The Girl on the Train" by Paula Hawkins
30. "The Light Between Oceans" by M.L. Stedman
31. "The Woman in the Window" by A.J. Finn
32. "The Bell Jar" by Sylvia Plath
33. "Pride and Prejudice" by Jane Austen
34. "The Awakening" by Kate Chopin
35. "The Color Purple" by Alice Walker
36. "The Secret Life of Bees" by Sue Monk Kidd
37. "The Joy Luck Club" by Amy Tan
38. "Persepolis" by Marjane Satrapi
39. "Eleanor Oliphant Is Completely Fine" by Gail Honeyman
40. "The Seven Husbands of Evelyn Hugo" by Taylor Jenkins Reid

This list includes a mix of classic feminist literature, contemporary works, and fiction that explores themes of female empowerment. It offers a diverse range of perspectives and stories to inspire and empower readers of all backgrounds.

Did you love *Boundless Trailblazers: Inspiring Stories of Real Women Throughout History*? Then you should read *The Art of Cozy: A Guide to Embracing Hygge for a Happier Life*[1] by Maarja Peebo!

[2]

Discover the secret to a happier, more fulfilling life with "The Art of Cozy: A guide to embracing hygge." This groundbreaking eBook by acclaimed author Maarja Peebo takes you on a journey to embrace the Danish concept of "hygge," a uniquely Scandinavian approach to living that emphasizes comfort, warmth, and an appreciation for life's simple pleasures.

In this book, Peebo provides practical, easy-to-follow guidance for incorporating the hygge lifestyle into your daily routine. You'll learn how to create a cozy home environment, prepare comforting meals, and practice mindfulness and self-care techniques that promote inner peace

1. https://books2read.com/u/baBLWP

2. https://books2read.com/u/baBLWP

and balanced well-being. Whether you're looking for ways to reduce stress, increase happiness, or simply add a touch of warmth to your daily life, "The Art of Cozy" is the key to unlocking the hygge lifestyle and discovering the true meaning of contentment.

So why wait? If you're ready to live a happier, more fulfilling life, order your copy of "The Art of Cozy" today and start your journey to embracing hygge!

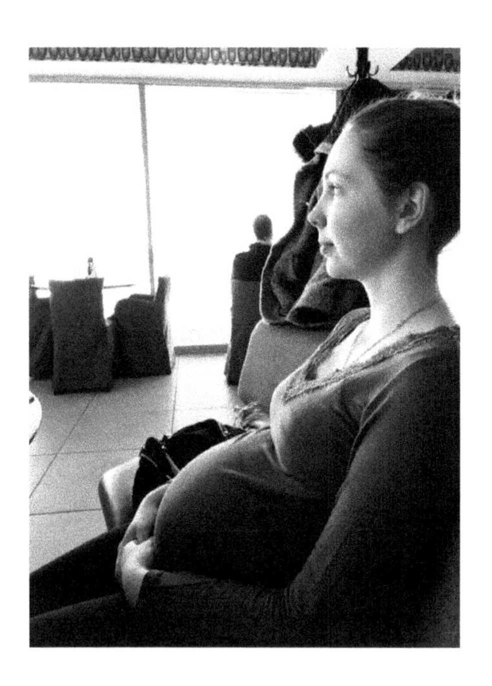

About the Author

Maarja Hammerberg, a dedicated mother of three young daughters, is on a mission to inspire and empower not only her children but the world. As a history graduate from the University of Tallinn, Maarja's passion for stories and the incredible women who have shaped history has always burned brightly.

Motivated by a desire to give her daughters the best start in life, Maarja has embarked on a journey to celebrate the achievements of remarkable women throughout history and the present. Her commitment to providing strong role models for her children and future generations serves as the foundation for her work.

When Maarja isn't busy being a loving and nurturing stay-at-home mom, she is a storyteller and advocate for women's empowerment. Through her writing, she aspires to kindle the same spark of determination, resilience, and courage in her daughters that has fueled her exploration of the unbreakable spirit of women throughout time.

With Maarja Hammerberg, the stories of incredible women are

not just tales from the past but beacons of inspiration for a boundless future.